CONSENSUS IN THE CLASSROOM

CONSENSUS IN THE CLASSROOM

Fostering A Lively Learning Community

LINDA SARTOR, Ph.D.
and
MOLLY YOUNG BROWN, M.A.

Published by Psychosynthesis Presss in collaboration with Consensus Classroom, Inc.

Psychosynthesis Press, PO Box 1301, Mt. Shasta, CA 96067, (530) 926-0986
books@mollyyoungbrown.com
http://www.mollyyoungbrown.com/books.htm

Consensus Classroom, Inc., 7899 St. Helena Rd., Santa Rosa, CA 95404
(707) 538-5123
Lsartor@inreach.com
http://home.inreach.com/lsartor

Cover and book design by Gabriel Graubner, The Electronic Monastery, 7899 St. Helena Road, Santa Rosa, CA 95404

Typography: Adobe Garamond, Friz Quadrata and Old Style MT

Cover Stock: 80lb. Cover/ 10pt, white acid-free matte coated finish sheet; text paper: Trade book opaque, 444ppi Crème acid free

Printed by Lightning Source, Inc., 1246 Heil Quaker Blvd, Lavergne, TN 37086

Cover and title page photographs by Sandy and Mac Thomson.
Classroom photographs by Gabe Fraire

ISBN 0-9611444-4-0

Copyright © Linda Sartor and Molly Brown, 2004, all rights reserved

First Printing 2004 in the United States of America

Acknowledgements

We want to acknowledge a few of the people who have supported us in writing this book. Most importantly, we want to thank Linda's students whose stories fill these pages.

We acknowledge Linda's first co-author, Helen Loceff (who later changed her name to Ariel Ray). For many years, Linda only talked about her experience with using consensus decision-making in her classrooms. During that time, many people asked for something in writing and Linda always said, "But I'm not a writer." Helen's response to this was, "Well, I am." So Helen really gave birth to the first version of this book, which captured Linda's experiences in writing. That unpublished manuscript documented many stories that otherwise would have been forgotten and lost during the years that passed before Molly and Linda began to work on this book.

We also want to acknowledge and thank our readers, Rebecca Beyman, Carroll Hirsch, Mary Hutchings, and Jack Travis, who each did a careful and thoughtful reading of the new manuscript and gave valuable feedback towards making this final version more reader and teacher friendly.

Graphic artist Gabriel Graubner designed the book beautifully. Board members of the non-profit organization, Consensus Classroom Inc, have been supporting this endeavor all along. They include: Rebecca Beyman, Richard Dale, Mary Gomes, Jurgen Kremer, Peter Laughingwolf, Robert Paton, Peter Wood, and Marybeth Ventura. We also want to appreciate Gabe Fraire and the children in Linda's classroom for the classroom photographs, as well as Sandy and Mac Thomson and the children of Heartwood Cohousing for the cover and title page photographs. Finally, Molly wants to thank her husband, Jim, for overall moral support and feedback on specific sections.

Because the writing took place over a number of years, there were many other people in our lives who also provided support in many ways and on many levels. We extend our gratitude to them as well.

Table of Contents

Foreword v

Introduction 1
About the authors: Linda; Molly. Overview. Using Linda's voice. Two caveats.

**Chapter 1: Consensus Decision-making
for a Humane, Sustainable Culture** 9
What is consensus? Common concerns about using consensus: *time; power differentials; academic performance.* Consensus decision-making for healthy systems.

**Chapter 2: Democracy in Action:
Benefits of Consensus in the Classroom** 21
Shared authority and responsibility: *opportunities for student leadership, inner authority and interpersonal conflict.* Enhanced self-expression: *feelings matter; speaking up; feeling understood; love.* Full participation. Creative decision-making. Conscious community: *conscious community supports its members; consensus practice supports conscious community.*

**Chapter 3: Consensus and Community Building:
Practices from Linda's Classroom** 43
Class Meetings: *agenda; decision-making.* Leadership: *hand-raising; majority vote.* Interpersonal relationships: *the disturbance rule; a simple conflict resolution process; put-downs and name-calling.* Court system: *a few court cases.* Money system: *how we did it one year.* Decisions about homework. The listening game.

Chapter 4: Consensus in Post-Modern Education 61
Authority, democracy, and individual choice: *authority; democracy; choice.* New pedagogical understandings and challenges: *brain research; inquiry, action and reflection; a paradigm shift for curriculum.* Creating cooperative and multicultural learning communities: *caring and "voice"; building learning communities; cooperative learning; consensus vs. majority vote in class meetings.* The emerging paradigm in post-modern education.

Chapter 5: Getting Started 83
Getting the idea accepted in the culture of the school. Introducing consensus: *yurt circle; introducing consensus through the homework decision; the first class meeting; common vision.* Common challenges: *the inevitable long meeting; stuck in the muck; the Blocker.* Shifting from being the authority to sharing the authority. Encouraging self-expression. Process and outcomes. Consensus resources.

Afterword 97

Appendix: Katherine Kennedy–Another Teacher's Story 99
Katherine's report. Katherine's journal.

References 119

Index 123

*This book is dedicated
to the memory of
Rebecca Beyman,
loving teacher who gave
so much of herself to so many.*

Foreword

One of the single most important things we can do with our students is talk with them–talk with them, not to or at them. It takes courage and structure. It takes skill and practice. In this book, the authors share their process for engaging young people in real problem-solving discussion. They inspire and edify. They open the doors to their classrooms and invite us in. We come away more knowledgeable and better able to go to work.

The value of holding class meetings is now well documented. Teachers plan events, decide on class rules, prepare for substitute teachers, or name their pets using this format. They also invite their students to help figure out safer ways to play at recess, or how to resolve conflicts. Using class meetings and consensus decision-making, teachers can guide and facilitate a democratic process that develops and encourages critical thinking, perspective, and empathy. It is–as these writer-teachers assert–an essential part of building community and citizenship.

And then the authors take it further. They confront the big old snag. As kids get older they get better and better at telling us what they think we want to hear. As a colleague puts it, "They can talk the talk even if they have no intention of walking the walk." How do we allow for honest dialogue and active listening while confronting real issues, issues that trigger our own very strong beliefs?

In this case, the authors are deeply concerned about the environment. They note how easily children are moved to save the rainforest or recycle, how quickly they sign up for such projects. But in-between the seams of good intentions and assignments, we see the coke cans tossed on the ground. How do we really get children thinking and doing, taking on issues beyond easy compliance?

Faced at times with disappointment in our students, we may resort again to the reflex lecture and sermon rather than sustain the conversation. The conversation, we learn in this study, is often moved to the next level through a process of consensus. It is here that lip-service or surface responses are confronted and pondered, that students engage each other in stretching their perspectives.

As this book suggests, this requires a shift in our own approaches as we learn to trust the children and our tools.

This book offers background and context. It offers lively illustration. And, importantly, it offers the wisdom of wonderful teachers.

Ruth S. Charney
Greenfield Massachusetts

Teacher for over thirty years
Co-Founder of Northeast Foundation for Children and
    Greenfield Center School
Author of *Teaching Children To Care*

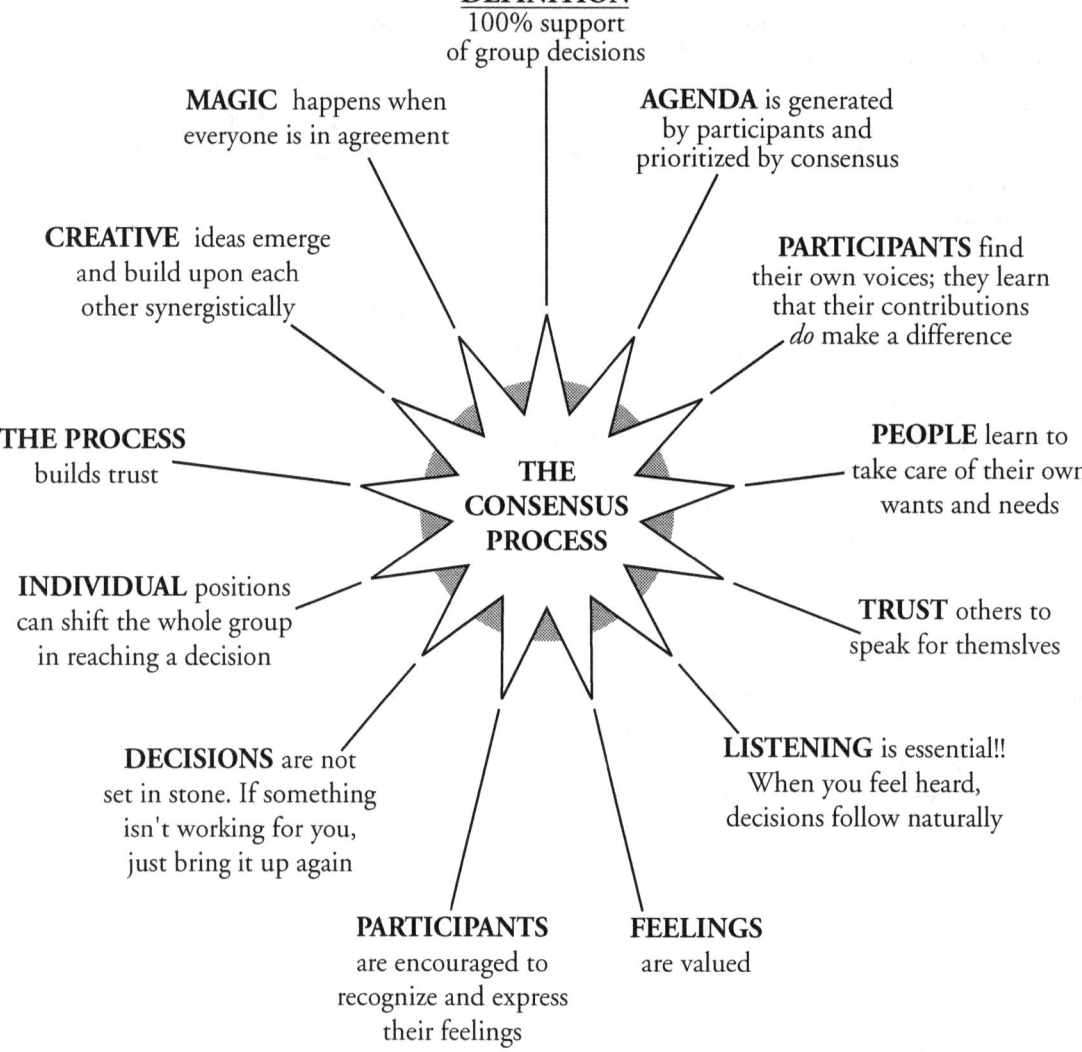

Introduction

Consensus decision-making is a dynamic and democratic approach to creating a true learning community in the classroom. The key to a vibrant consensus is the acceptance and validation of each person's point of view and way of operating in the world, which we believe will help build a more democratic, sustainable, and intelligent society. Although the experience reported in this book took place in a self-contained classroom, we believe this approach can be useful for teachers and classrooms at all levels, in all kinds of school settings. To begin, we introduce ourselves and offer an overview of the book.

About the Authors

Linda Sartor ✻ A graduate program in environmental education provided my first experience of participating in a consensus decision-making community. Prior to graduate school, I taught sixth grade and was a part of a team developing an environmental education curriculum that included a week long residential camp. Despite the enthusiasm we teachers had for the topic, and our holistic and integrated curriculum design, I was not seeing any real changes in my students in terms of living more ecological lives at school and at home. In the unique graduate program with the Audubon Expedition Institute, I realized that engagement in the consensus process might be a key to providing environmental education that would really make a difference in our human relationship with the earth as a living system. So I decided to try using consensus decision-making with my students when I returned to the classroom. My experience doing so over the subsequent seven years provides the substance of this book.

Coming home from the Audubon Expedition, I moved into Monan's Rill, an intentional community based on a sense of extended family, and stewardship of the land. Here I became part of a Quaker-influenced consensus decision-making process. This community continues to be central to my life.

I have enjoyed participating in a great variety of other consensus communities with children and adults, for short and long terms, in small and large groups. These have included weekend workshops, graduate courses and programs, on-going research and learning collectives, a spiritual community, and large civil disobedience demonstrations. My doctoral dissertation, *Facilitating Collaboration* (1998), focuses on a model for equalizing the power dynamics within collaborating groups. Moreover, I usually seek other people's perspectives even when making personal decisions, because I believe I make wiser decisions that way. Through all these experiences in and out of the classroom, consensus decision-making has become an integral part of my life.

Currently I teach in several graduate schools: a teaching credential program, a master's degree program in ecological teaching and learning, and a cultural consciousness project. I also guide desert wilderness experiences that include a three-day solo fast for people in transition seeking wisdom from within themselves and from nature.

Molly Young Brown ❋ Although my background includes several years of classroom teaching and group facilitation, my primary experience with consensus–prior to meeting Linda–was in activist organizations. One group had been  using a sloppy version of "Robert's Rules of Order" and decided to try consensus because we believed it to be more aligned with our philosophy than majority rule. Unfortunately, none of us really had a clue about how consensus works, so our meetings rapidly disintegrated into debates in which people on one side of an issue would try to convince those on the other side, for hours on end. Unfortunately, those who could hold out the longest, or the bias of the person leading the discussion, would often determine the decision. I know now we did not understand the radically different approach that consensus requires: a sincere desire on the part of the participants (and especially the facilitator) to examine and include all points of view, rather than to simply persuade one group to go along with another.

I met Linda when my husband Jim and I began visiting the intentional community where she lives. I was exposed to a more workable version of consensus at the same time I got to know Linda. Later Linda, Jim, and I worked together on a project called "Peace in Our Schools" and I learned more about Linda's work with consensus in the classroom, eventually auditing her college course on the subject. I served on the Board for Consensus Classroom, Inc, promoting the concept through the videotape and workbook Linda had created, both entitled "The Consensus Classroom." When Linda asked for help revising the workbook to create this current book, I gladly volunteered, having recently completed another co-authoring effort with Joanna Macy *(Coming Back to Life, 1998)*.

After the writing project was underway, Jim and I moved to another intentional community governed by consensus: Heartwood Cohousing in Bayfield, Colorado. I became even more firmly committed to this decision-making process, acting as one of the group of facilitators for business meetings. A speaker at the North American Cohousing Conference 2001 said that consensus decision-making is the single most important contribution that cohousing is making to cultural transformation in North America and elsewhere. I have to agree. Writing this book with Linda has been philosophically satisfying as well as personally enjoyable.

My central concern these days is how we in the industrialized world can come to understand ourselves as part of the interdependent web of life, and begin to act like responsible members of that web. I believe passionately that we need to develop respect for all the diverse expressions of life, and their interrelationships. I believe that consensus decision-making takes us in that direction: we learn to respect the diversity of perspectives of our fellow humans in the process of coming to decisions that work for everyone. In all our decisions, in and out of the classroom, may we also learn to take into account the needs and inherent value of other life forms with which we share this precious planet.

Overview

We begin in Chapter 1 by describing the context for consensus in today's world, and our vision for what consensus decision-making might do to transform our society into a more humane and sustainable culture. We explore the meaning of consensus, especially as distinguished from agreement, compromise, and conformity. We look at common concerns about consensus, such as time use and power differentials. Applying principles of systems thinking, we explore how the process of consensus decision-making supports the development of healthy social systems.

Chapter 2 describes the benefits and dynamics of consensus that Linda experienced in her classroom, including shared authority and responsibility, enhanced self-expression, full participation, creative decision-making, and the building of an increasingly conscious community. We see this chapter as pivotal to the whole book; if a reader were to read only one chapter, this would be the one we recommend.

In Chapter 3, we describe in more detail some of the specific practices that emerged in Linda's consensus classroom. One was central to the way she facilitated consensus decision-making (class meetings), and some arose fairly spontaneously out of the process (the "disturbance agreement," a court system, a money system, "the homework decision," and a listening game). We include these latter practices for their potential usefulness to other teachers and classes. We see them as congruent with the consensus process, but do not want to imply that they are essential to it.

> TEACHERS NEED TO BE WILLING TO SHARE SOME OF THEIR TRADITIONAL AUTHORITY WITH THEIR STUDENTS.

In Chapter 4, we summarize post-modern educational theory and practices that support the use of consensus in the classroom. We begin by describing the post-modern paradigm shift as we understand it. We survey many educational theories regarding authority, democracy, and individual choice. We explore a variety of pedagogical insights and challenges that have emerged in cooperative and multicultural learning communities. We end with an overview of the emerging paradigm in post-modern education and how consensus decision-making supports that paradigm. We include this information for those readers who want to broaden their understanding of our theoretical framework.

In Chapter 5, we offer some suggestions for getting started using consensus in your own classroom. We explore the challenge of securing acceptance of the idea in the culture of the school through communicating with site administrators, parents, and colleagues. We suggest ways to introduce consensus to a class: the Yurt Circle, the decision about homework, the first class meeting, and creating a "Shared Vision." Then we explore challenges commonly faced in the beginning (even when the teacher is experienced with consensus): the "Inevitable Long Meeting," "Stuck in the Muck," and the "Blocker." We go on to discuss one of the biggest challenges many teachers face: shifting from being the authority to sharing the authority. And lastly, we suggest some practical ways to encourage student self-expression—so necessary to the consensus process.

> WE WANT ONLY TO INSPIRE YOU TO TRY IT OUT, IN YOUR OWN WAY AND STYLE, WITH YOUR OWN FLAVOR.

For a delightful, heart-warming account of one other teacher's experience implementing consensus in her classroom, we recommend you read the Appendix. "Katherine Kennedy: Another Teacher's Story" includes her report and journal about teaching third grade at an international school in Finland.

Using Linda's Voice

In writing the book, we faced an interesting dilemma. Both of us have strong ideas and perspectives to contribute to the book, and want to speak with a common voice. At the same time, we are drawing primarily on Linda's experience in public school classrooms, at the second and sixth grade levels. When we wrote of her experience, we did not want to use a rather awkward third person, referring to "Linda's idea" or "Linda's feeling." So when we describe her particular experience, we usually use her voice in the first person. Molly has contributed to the writing of those sections, too, but the experiences—and the voice—are Linda's.

Two Caveats

We state now—as we will several times throughout the book—one of our central concerns. We believe that there are as many right ways to do consensus as there are groups who have developed this decision-making strategy, and we want to encourage each of you—in collaboration with your students—to find your own way to do it. So please do not construe anything we say in this book—any suggestion we make or stories we recount—to be a prescription for the "Right Way" to do consensus. We want only to inspire you to try it out, in your own way and style, with your own flavor. The experiences shared here took place mainly in self-contained elementary school classrooms. Teachers working in secondary and college settings will no doubt have to make more radical adaptations to the practices described here.

We believe, however, that there are certain essentials for teachers bringing consensus to their classrooms. Teachers need to be willing: to share some of their traditional authority with their students, to listen well to their students, and to abide by the decisions made in this way. (Of course a teacher, or anyone else, can always reopen a decision for further consideration, when the decision does not seem to work, or has unintended consequences). Because consensus decision-making moves a community in the direction of democracy, shared power and authority, and mutual respect and consideration, teachers believing in a strong authoritarian approach will find consensus unsettling at best-if not downright subversive. However, such teachers are unlikely to be attracted to this book in the first place. Having picked it up, you are doubtlessly inclined to a more democratic classroom already, and are seeking ways to support that inclination without creating a chaotic or overly permissive atmosphere in your classroom. You are the teacher for whom we have written this book, and we hope you will find that using a consensus process fits your needs and values.

Through the consensus process, teachers can gain a broader understanding of their students' needs, abilities, and concerns, so that even their "top down" decisions will be more informed. Students learn how to participate more fully and responsibly in their classrooms, acquiring skills and attitudes that will serve them well elsewhere in life. In turn, our society as a whole benefits from more of its members prepared—and even expecting—to participate fully in the critical decisions we face.

CHAPTER 1

Consensus Decision-making for a Humane Sustainable Culture

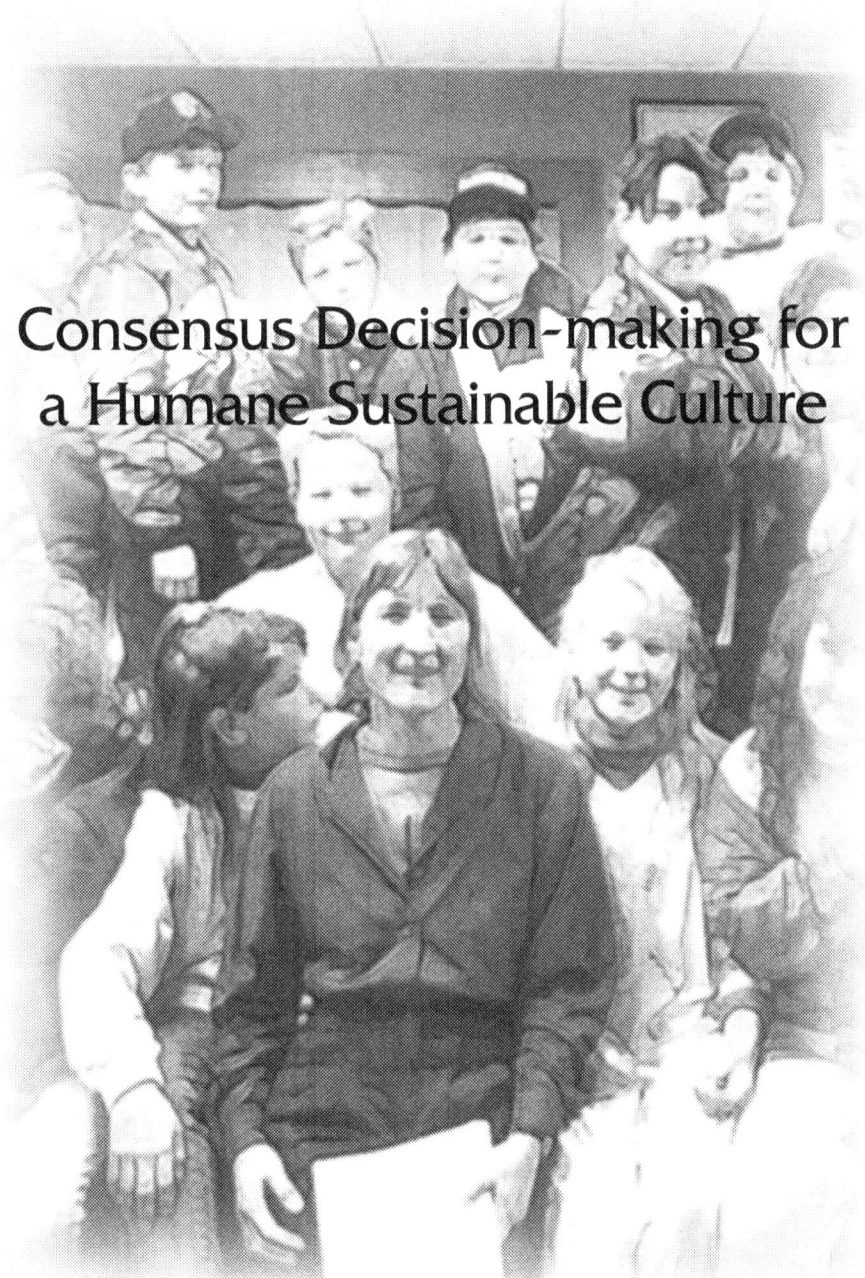

Consensus Decision-making for a Humane Sustainable Culture

How we make decisions within any group or social system deeply affects the health of that system. Iroquois and other indigenous peoples have used forms of consensus decision-making for many generations. However, other peoples–including the Indo-Europeans–have made decisions in ways that ignore the needs and wisdom of large parts of our social systems, thus disenfranchising and oppressing individuals and groups. For a long time, kings and other hierarchical authorities decided from the top what was best for the society. In the last few hundred years, some Western societies began to experiment with various forms of majority rule. Majority rule at least attempts to acknowledge the rights and wisdom of the people making up the society, assuming that what the majority wants is probably the best thing to do. However, majority rule imposes its own tyranny upon the minority, tending to suppress the voices of those who view things differently. Until recently, only a few groups in the industrialized world–such as the Quakers–have practiced consensus, seeking decisions that honor everyone's ideas and concerns.

Today we face grave crises in the world. Our current ways of doing business are destroying whole species and ecosystems around the planet, as we use up resources to feed an unsustainable economy. Military systems around the globe–used to gain or maintain power–kill millions and sometimes destroy whole cultures. Many children are growing up fearful and hopeless, driving some to further acts of violence. It appears that the dominant culture of our world needs to act far more intelligently and harmoniously if we want to survive and thrive as a species.

We desperately need decision-making processes that bring forth the creativity and intelligence of everyone in order to solve the grave problems before us. We the authors believe that consensus decision-making–skillfully and honestly used–can meet this need on a small scale, and open up the possibility of collaborative decision-making on a global scale. And what better place to begin practicing than our classrooms?

What Is Consensus?

The media sometimes uses the word "consensus" to indicate a trend of agreement that might not include everyone–in other words, the majority opinion–and this can be confusing. For the purposes of this book, we define consensus as conscious agreement by everyone. Under this definition, a decision is not final until everyone in the group agrees with it. We call the interaction that leads to consensus–or at least attempts to find consensus–the "consensus process."

In our understanding, the spirit of consensus holds that authority lies in the group, so we recommend that any group seeking to use consensus develop its own definition—by consensus! Even if a group were to begin with our definition, there would still be many nuances with which to work. What does "agreement by everyone" mean? In some groups, it may mean that everyone has had the opportunity to say "no," and silence is interpreted as agreement. In other groups, it may mean that interaction continues until everyone actually says "yes." In her classroom, Linda always asked for a show of hands to check on agreement, so everyone had to actively participate, at least to the level of choosing whether or not to raise a hand. Some groups, such as Molly's cohousing community, make use of colored cards. When checking for consensus, everyone holds up a color representing his or her opinion: green for agreement, red for disagreement, or orange for consent but with a concern to be heard.

> CONSENSUS DECISION-MAKING INVOLVES A WHOLLY DIFFERENT WAY OF THINKING.

Agreement does not have to mean that everyone is wildly excited about the decision. Quakers, who have practiced consensus for generations, provide for people to "stand aside" when they do not completely agree with a decision, but believe they can live with it. In Molly's community, people holding up an orange card bow to the wisdom of the group, without giving up their own unique perspective and preference. They are asking that their concerns be heard, but not necessarily resolved. Even so, stating the concern may lead to further discussion. In the classroom, students (or the teacher) who object to a decision have the opportunity to consider and articulate their concerns—it is not enough to just say "no."

Other consensus groups believe that everyone has to give a solid "yes," so standing aside is not an option. Such groups keep discussing and resolving any hesitancy on the part of their members before finalizing a decision. Attention to hesitancy may surface a hidden issue to examine, leading to a better decision. Linda's approach—asking students to raise their hands to indicate their agreement—usually surfaced any hesitancy.

Although each decision is important, getting to closure on a decision is not the only priority; of equal importance is the problem-solving process that considers everyone's needs and perspectives. Consensus decision-making involves a wholly different way of thinking. Rather than trying to impose one set of concerns over another, or trying to negotiate a compromise, consensus requires a creative group process, in which all participants are invested in accommodating everyone's needs. Participants listen and speak with the intention to reach a decision that satisfies everyone's needs and values. When decisions are approached with this attitude, amazing new solutions emerge.

We have noticed that many people think consensus means compromise, but in our experience, consensus differs significantly from compromise. In compromise, people who are in disagreement about an issue each agree to sacrifice something in order to reach a decision that is tolerable to everyone. We see consensus, on the other hand, as a synergistic decision-making process that includes all concerns, needs, and perspectives without sacrifice—and in so doing, leads to a better decision than anyone might have conceived on his/her own. Often in a consensus discussion, a new solution emerges that satisfies what previously appeared to be diametrically opposed needs or perspectives. There is then no need for compromise, and the resulting decision is the best for everyone concerned. Moreover, students learn first-hand the power of cooperation.

Common Concerns about Using Consensus in the Classroom

Consensus sometimes has a bad reputation in spite of its philosophical appeal. Consensus may be confused with a false unanimity accomplished by social pressure and the subtle suppression of dissent. Or it may be seen as an endless debate that only ends when one or the other side gives up. Consensus may seem more frustrating and inefficient than the more familiar forms of decision-making. This does not mean, however, that we should give it up. As in any discipline, we need to develop the requisite skills.

Time

Consensus can be time-consuming, especially when a group is first learning how to work in this way. Sometimes a group gets bogged down in endless discussion without ever coming to a satisfactory decision. The group may then end up using majority vote just to move ahead, abandoning the consensus process. Given sufficient skill and structure, however, the consensus process need take no longer than the debate often involved in majority rule. In classrooms, students may enjoy the process so much that they work actively to make it succeed. And with everyone concerned "buying into" the decision, the actual implementation of it can be more efficient, since there is no disaffected minority left to complain, slow things down, or otherwise subvert the implementation. Furthermore, because the discussion leading to consensus is more likely to include all concerns, fewer unanticipated roadblocks occur.

> STUDENTS LEARN FIRST-HAND THE POWER OF COOPERATION.

Successful consensus requires skill as well as structure. Participants have to listen in a deeper way to each other's perspectives and needs, not as debate points to be countered, but as concerns to be creatively addressed and included. Old habits such as "one-upsmanship" die hard, so the consensus process is always a learning process. As in any group using consensus, students develop self-reflective skills, learning to consider the usefulness to the group of an intended remark–or of keeping silent. One learns to ask, "Will this remark further our group thinking on the subject?" or "How will my concern help shape the decision for the benefit of all, including myself?"

Some groups select members to serve as facilitators who structure and focus the discussion. Facilitators may point out when the discussion wanders onto issues not essential to the topic at hand. Molly's community uses colored cards during discussion in a different way than when checking for agreement. The cards indicate to the facilitator the nature of participants' contributions: question (yellow), information (green), comment or opinion (blue). In classrooms, the teacher needs facilitation skills (which may be somewhat distinct from other teaching skills), and may train students to facilitate as well. In the authors' experience, the process of consensus decision-making becomes more efficient as the group and its facilitators develop the requisite skills.

Power Differentials

Another concern is that consensus decision-making is vulnerable to manipulation. Can someone block a decision by refusing to resolve a concern or continually bringing up new ones? Can an outspoken person persuade others to go along with his/her preferred decision through innuendo and convincing half-truths? Can someone influence decisions by subtle put-downs of differing points of view, or by engendering social pressure towards one "politically correct" point of view?

Certainly all these power plays can occur. Consensus decision-making is no panacea for human vice. However, as we will show in our exploration throughout this book, the consensus process actually makes it much less likely that these kinds of manipulations will occur. First of all, people find it unnecessary to resort to such tactics, because they know their concerns and needs will be heard and included. Individuals often feel more empowered through consensus, and people are encouraged–indeed expected–to speak up when something seems unfair, misleading, or otherwise uncomfortable. And because feelings are valued as carrying important information, participants can comment that something "just doesn't feel right" and expect a more sympathetic hearing than they would in a debate. We believe, in fact, that the practice of consensus decision-making over time–and in more and more groups and classrooms–would raise the quality of communication in general to new levels of honesty and intelligence.

Academic Performance

Teachers today are under a lot of pressure to assure a high level of academic performance on the part of their students as measured by standardized tests. It may seem that consensus decision-making would take valuable time away from preparing one's students for such tests. Although we have not attempted to scientifically measure the effects of the consensus process on performance on standardized tests, current brain research and learning theory support the use of this approach.

Joseph Chilton Pearce (1991, 2002) has integrated much of current brain and learning research in several books. He describes how fear and stress stimulate the reptilian brain or R-system, undermining higher brain functions of the neocortex. The reptilian brain has a very limited range of response to perceived threat: fight or flight. When fear activates that part of our brain, we can't think clearly or creatively. We rely on old patterns and can only learn in the most rudimentary way, by rote and reflex.

> A negative experience of any kind, whether an event in our environment or simply a thought in our head, brings an automatic shift of attention and energy from our forebrain to our hindbrain—that is, away from our higher verbal-intellectual brain toward the lower R-system and its defenses. This shift shortchanges our intellect, cripples our learning and memory, and can lock our neocortex into service of our lowest brain. (Pearce, p. 33)

Pearce comments, "It is interesting to note that testing is interpreted by all of us as a judgmental threat and shifts our energy and attention from the emotional-cognitive brain and prefrontals to the R-system [reptilian brain], which compromises whatever higher intellect we may have" (2002, p. 113). So anything we teachers can do to mitigate this perceived threat should help improve student performance on tests.

Furthermore, when children feel safe and loved, they follow nature's plan to develop their higher intelligences. As described in Chapter 2, classrooms based on consensus decision-making can provide an environment in which every child feels respected, affirmed, and safe. According to Pearce's arguments, such children will naturally and eagerly learn—whatever the curriculum offered to them. Moreover, they have in the consensus process itself the requisite models for developing critical, creative thinking, an essential basis of a sound education.

Consensus Decision Making for Healthy Systems

Understanding how social systems operate in terms of consensus—and developing practices accordingly—can help mitigate the problems of time and power misuse. In our view, consensus requires a paradigm shift in how people think about themselves and their relationships to one another. We believe consensus works because we humans are so radically interdependent with one another that anything one person does at someone else's expense ultimately damages the health of the larger system that sustains everyone. Moreover, we see that participating in the consensus process reaffirms that each person's welfare is inextricably entangled with the welfare of everyone else (and with the welfare of all the living systems on the planet). From this perspective, consensus in one form or another seems more likely to ensure the common weal than majority rule or top-down decision-making.

> ...THE CONSENSUS PROCESS REAFFIRMS THAT EACH PERSON'S WELFARE IS INEXTRICABLY ENTANGLED WITH THE WELFARE OF EVERYONE ELSE.

Arising out of the biological sciences, General Systems Theory (Laszlo, 1972; Macy, 1991; Capra, 1996) attempts to map general principles for how all systems work, especially living systems. The Cartesian approach examines phenomena by attempting to break things down into component parts; General Systems Theory (GST) explores phenomena in terms of dynamic patterns of relationship. This shift in focus—from entities frozen in time to dynamic relationships—underlies systems thinking.

When we look at consensus in the light of some of the principles that systems theorists have articulated, we begin to appreciate why consensus supports healthy human systems. We can also deepen our understanding of what consensus really is, and how it can best function.

Systems theorists have noticed that four patterns of relationship and information flow—called "invariants"—seem to inhere in all living systems, whether one-celled bacteria, trees, human bodies, or ecosystems: 1) nested hierarchy; 2) synergy or emergent properties; 3) homeostasis, and 4) adaptation. (see Figure 1)

Figure 1

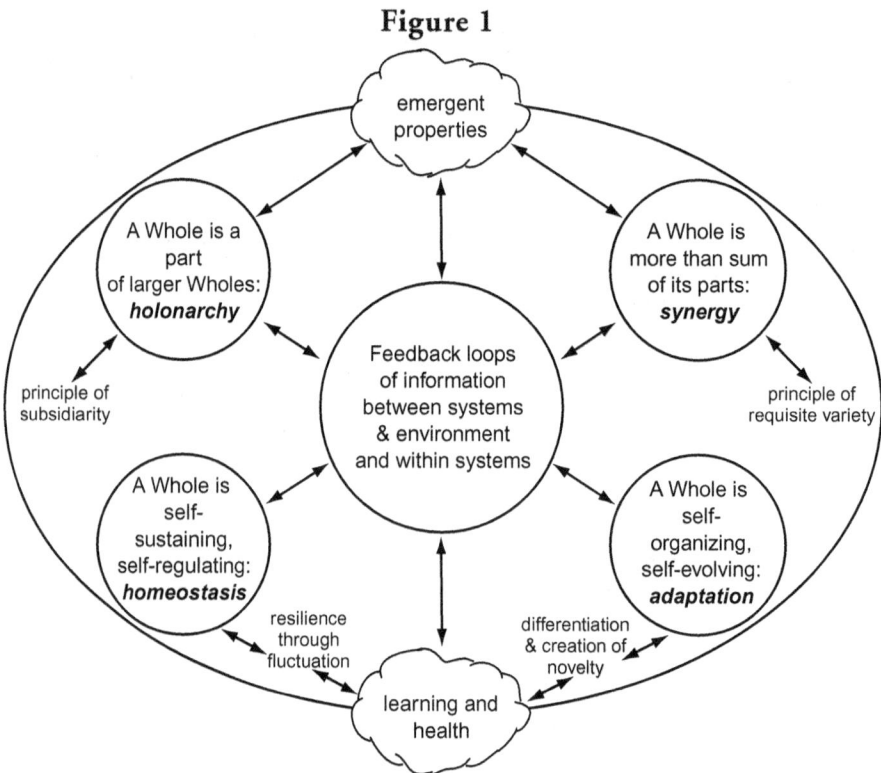

Systems function through dynamic patterns of information flow and relationship

Invariant 1 ※ Every system is made up of subsystems and in turn holds membership in one or more larger systems, forming a kind of nested hierarchy—systems within systems. This is not the kind of hierarchy in which one individual rules at the top. Instead, the collective membership of a system governs the whole through an intricate web of interrelationships and information exchange. Every Whole (holon) is a part of larger Wholes, hence the term *"holonarchy."*

If we applied this model to education, we would encourage all levels and parts of the system—students, teachers, and administrators—to contribute to decision-making. Since our current school system still operates under the top-down model of authority, the classroom teacher must work within the framework defined by state, district, and school policies. However, the teacher can shift the model of hierarchy within his/her classroom, and guide students toward class "holonarchy."

Invariant 2 ❊ As the old saying goes, "the whole is more than the sum of its parts." So at each new level of systemic organization, unpredictable properties and capacities emerge: "emergent properties" or *synergy* in action. For example, a human being is something more than just a conglomerate of carbon, oxygen, and hydrogen, mixed in with a few other elements. A human is even more than a conglomerate of cells and tissues. How these ingredients are *organized* makes for humanness, and for the distinctiveness of each individual human as well.

Consensus allows synergy to occur, because it allows for the full participation of all of a system's members. Through the dialogue that occurs in coming to consensus, the wisdom of the class as a whole can emerge, rather than be limited to one or two choices presented by the teacher. New ideas and creative solutions can (and often do) emerge from the class, beyond anything any one individual member, even the teacher, might have invented.

When we use majority rule, we may suppress the very real needs and wisdom of one of our members, and the health of the whole system may suffer as a consequence. It is like letting the skin cells determine the right way to be a cell, because they are more numerous than the cells that exchange oxygen and carbon dioxide in the lungs.

> BECAUSE DECISIONS CANNOT BE MADE WITHOUT THE AGREEMENT OF EVERYONE INVOLVED, ATTENTION MUST BE PAID TO EVERYONE'S NEEDS, CONCERNS, AND PERSPECTIVES.

The third and fourth invariants have to do with how systems respond to change.

Invariant 3 ❊ Living systems maintain their form over time in a kind of fluctuating balance (called *"homeostasis"*). Each Whole is self-sustaining and self-regulating, providing a resilience through all the internal and external fluctuations inherent in life. A consensus classroom encourages a high level of individual responsibility, so each student can self-regulate, rather than being constantly directed by the teacher.

Invariant 4 ❊ At the same time, systems adapt themselves to changes in their environment. Each Whole is therefore self-organizing, and self-evolving: *adaptation* occurs constantly. Because of the communication and interaction that occurs in a consensus classroom, students have manifold opportunities to take in new information and reorganize themselves accordingly. Some information may reinforce existing beneficial patterns of thought and behavior (self-regulation) while other information may require a new understanding and a new behavioral response (self-organization). Systems maintain health–and learn–by means of these two invariants.

Living systems perform these miraculous tasks by receiving information from their environment and from within, comparing it to their established "codes" (acquired through genetics and/or previous learning) and responding accordingly. This process is called feedback, which has a very specific meaning in General Systems Theory (GST). Because feedback is circular–information from the environment evoking a response from the system, and the response in turn affecting the relationship of the system to the environment–GST considers feedback to occur in " loops."

Information flow is of paramount importance to both homeostasis and adaptation. Any system needs constant information from all its parts about how they are functioning and what signals they are picking up from the environment. Otherwise the system's responses may not fit the changing needs of the system within its ever-changing environment.

Consensus seems to offer great promise for this information flow. Because decisions cannot be made without the agreement of everyone involved, attention must be paid to everyone's needs, concerns, and perspectives. These in turn reflect the changing circumstances of the group/system–its internal relationships and its relationships to the world. When decisions are made from the top down, or even by majority rule, valuable information may be suppressed, ignored, or never even received by the decision-makers.

All four invariants also speak to the need for a consensus process in which group members or students are truly committed to finding solutions that meet everyone's needs, or at least take everyone's concerns into account. This commitment includes resisting pressure to come to premature decision, before all concerns have been aired. In order for synergy to work, all parts of the system must participate, at least by active acquiescence. Synergy is enhanced when even the quiet ones actively indicate their agreement with the decision by raising their hands, giving voice, or otherwise indicating their assent.

In GST, two principles complement the first two invariants (see Figure 1). The first principle–subsidiarity–indicates that decisions are best made at the lowest possible level within a nested hierarchy of systems. To extend the analogy of the human body, our organs, tissues, and cells make innumerable "decisions" every moment, as they respond to chemical and physical changes within our bodies. Although we like to think of our brains as running the whole show, they really don't. All cells, tissues, and organs operate as semi-autonomous systems even as they constantly interact and affect one another.

Similarly, consensus decisions need to be made at the level of the problem or question being addressed. A whole group doesn't need to come to consensus each time one of its members needs to get a drink of water, or go to the bathroom (although the group might want to set up logistical guidelines for these activities). Many decisions can and should be made at the level of the individual; only when a situation affects other people do those others need to be involved. Decisions or conflicts involving two people may be resolved between the two parties, sometimes calling upon a third person to act as mediator or consultant. However, if a conflict between two individuals begins to disturb and polarize a group, then the other members of the group may need to be involved in its solution.

The second principle—requisite variety—indicates that systems need variety within themselves in order to respond to a variety of demands from their environment. Eliciting a variety of perspectives from students allows for much richer possibilities than a single teacher can provide alone. Consensus encourages diversity, seeking out all the various perspectives of the group and finding a part for each member to play in decisions and solutions. So often the small dissenting voice brings in a truth that no one else has seen, stimulating a far more creative and effective solution than a homogenous group would have found.

Schools—and the classrooms within them-are social systems, among the most influential systems in our culture. Practicing consensus in the classroom can improve the quality of educational activities as well as their appropriateness to the students. Although teachers obviously have a special role to play in classroom management, they can encourage their students to make many decisions individually or together through consensus. And since in consensus the teacher's concerns must be considered along with everyone else's, no decisions can be made that are contrary to the policies and educational requirements of the school system as a whole, or to the teacher's level of comfort.

Through the consensus process, teachers can gain a broader understanding of their students' needs, abilities, and concerns, so that even their "top down" decisions will be more informed. Students learn how to participate more fully and responsibly in their classrooms, acquiring skills and attitudes that will serve them well elsewhere in life. In turn, our society as a whole benefits from more of its members prepared—and even expecting—to participate fully in the critical decisions we face.

Through developing and practicing consensus decision-making skills in the classroom, my students were empowered to speak up, to listen, to synthesize ideas, to have a sense for the whole community, and to recognize their own gifts—their wants, needs and feelings as well as their experiences, skills, abilities, and other resources—which contributed to the community. They not only felt included and important; they were! And they came to know that they could truly make a difference. Through the process of creating a classroom community using consensus decision-making, I believe my students came to experience the unity beneath the surface appearance of separateness, and developed a strong sense of personal and social responsibility to their communities outside the classroom.

CHAPTER 2

Democracy in Action:
Benefits of Consensus in the Classroom

Democracy in Action: Benefits of Consensus in the Classroom

Consensus decision-making bestows benefits to the teacher and students individually, and to the class as a whole. Instead of making all the decisions and trying to take care of everyone's needs, the teacher shares both that authority and that responsibility with the whole class. Innovative decisions that respond to the specific needs of the group members arise from this shared authority. Students develop their own personal authority and responsibility, thereby avoiding power struggles and victimhood. Students and teacher alike develop more trust in one another and expand their capacity for self-expression. Everyone benefits from full participation and creative decision-making, and the class moves toward conscious community. To illustrate these benefits in more detail, Linda tells her own story as a classroom teacher, in the first person.

Shared Authority and Responsibility

In my consensus classroom everyone had authority. Since no decision was made without everyone's agreement, each participant had veto power. In effect, everyone was president! Moreover, varying opportunities arose for different people to take leadership at different times.

I felt relaxed knowing I could count on my students to speak up for themselves if something was disturbing them. I did not have to carry the responsibility for everyone's comfort, but simply took care of myself and trusted the students to take care of themselves. We all came from this premise of self-responsibility as we responded to whatever situation arose—and the situations were always different, always alive. By participating in decisions, everyone knew why we had the agreements we had. When some did not keep an agreement, anyone could remind the offender about it. With this shared responsibility, I was freer to be myself, which was the best gift I could give to my students.

Participation in consensus decision-making empowered my students and me together to be responsible for our environment. We each took responsibility for ourselves by speaking up for our needs, interests and limitations. Students took responsibility for their education by participating in discussions on how to fulfill requirements. We all took responsibility for the classroom environment by coming to agreements that made it a comfortable place for everyone.

Encouraging everyone to be an authority allowed ideas to emerge that otherwise might never have had a chance. If it were up to me as "the authority" in the room to come up with all the ideas, we would be limited to my experience, memory and creativity. Allowing ideas from anyone in the room gave us thirty times more of a resource to draw upon. Moreover, these innovative decisions created opportunities for student leadership.

Opportunities for Student Leadership

Every year in my middle school classes, students decided by consensus to elect a president whose job was to lead class meetings. The president practiced a consensus-style of leadership–facilitating the decision-making rather than making the decisions for the group. Different personal styles emerged as students learned that there are many "right" ways to facilitate a meeting. By the response of the class, the student leaders learned what worked, and what did not. They received direct feedback when a technique or approach was not effective. For example, one class president, Angela, who was very bossy at first, received feedback at a few frustrating meetings, and then began to invite more input.

Two practices originated through consensus decisions made in one of my first consensus classes and then came to function in my classroom year after year: a class court and a money system. Both provided opportunities for student leadership. A judge presided over the court and the rest of the class was the jury, making decisions by consensus. A treasurer managed the bookkeeping and distribution of funds in the money system. Both were elected offices. (See Chapter 3 for more details)

Students in some of my middle school classrooms came up with another leadership role, that of teacher for an occasional lesson. One year, students expressed interest in more directed art instruction, and everyone agreed that Terry was a good artist. We decided that he would teach a series of drawing lessons once a week on Fridays. My style of teaching art was to provide materials and techniques and let the students create. In contrast, Terry took the class through the steps he used to draw a cartoon character, showing how to give the character different expressions and positions. This was a lesson my students would never have gotten from me. In addition to learning how to draw a cartoon character, they were empowered by having a peer in front of the class and learning from him. Moreover, Terry had the opportunity to share his expertise, to make his special contribution and be honored for it.

In my consensus classroom, students even conducted academic lessons. June, who was very good in math, explained to the rest of the class how to add fractions–the content of that day's math page. She demonstrated her own method and strategy. The class responded with respect and appreciation, and some students understood her explanation, while they had not yet understood mine. Miguel led a history lesson. He had different students read out loud from the book and then he conducted a discussion on the answers to the questions at the end of the chapter. When someone asked a question to which he did not know the answer, he said to the class, "Does anyone have an answer to that question?"

In that class, when we came to a consensus about students leading academic lessons, everyone wanted to make it work, and so they cooperated with each other. I sat down and became a student for the period. (They loved the idea that they could put my name on the board if I talked out of turn). The students who taught a lesson came away with a better understanding of the content taught and probably a new respect for what it takes to be a teacher.

Inner Authority and Interpersonal Conflict

Sharing authority provided students with many opportunities to develop a sense of inner authority. Through the experience of the consensus process, students learned to look inside to clarify their own wants and needs, so they could better articulate and advocate for them. When they heard each other's wants and needs, they discovered ways that everyone's needs could be met, without competition. They learned to focus on what really matters, rather than "winning" or "being right." By speaking clearly and listening respectfully, they were less likely to get caught up in power struggles or feel like victims. They discovered their own capacity to resolve interpersonal problems without having to appeal to me to decide what was "fair."

Authority emerged as a process more than a position. All the members became increasingly aware of the whole situation from their individual perspectives. Consensus discussion provided a remedy to the situation that occurs in the well-known parable of the "blind men and the elephant." In the story, each man reports what he perceives and assumes himself to be the authority on the whole elephant. In consensus, each man would communicate his perspective and listen to the others, so all would have a more complete sense of the elephant.

Sometimes students discovered later that they were not satisfied with a decision, and realized how they failed to speak up for their own wants and needs when the decision was under discussion. They often learned to check in more carefully with their inner authority about their wants and needs before agreeing with a decision another time.

When my students or I realized after the fact that we were not satisfied with a decision, we faced the dilemma of whether to live with it or bring it up for reconsideration. Either way, we practiced an important skill–either active acceptance or assertiveness–that helped us avoid feeling like victims.

I found that as the year progressed and each student learned to check in with his/her inner authority, I did not have to check out every decision with the class by asking for agreement. I could trust more and more that they would speak up when something was going on that conflicted with their wants or needs. So when someone asked me for permission to do something that would have an effect on others–such as setting up a project in a corner of the classroom–I would say, "It's okay with me as long as no one objects." If anyone did object, the students concerned could negotiate directly. Only if negotiation did not resolve the issue did we need to discuss it at a class meeting.

> THROUGH THE EXPERIENCE OF THE CONSENSUS PROCESS, STUDENTS LEARNED TO LOOK INSIDE TO CLARIFY THEIR OWN WANTS AND NEEDS...

Moving Beyond Power Struggles ❉ Power struggles occur when people are caught in what appears to be mutually exclusive positions. In my first year of teaching using the consensus process, I found myself in a power struggle with my principal that turned into a lesson for both my students and me. I hadn't said much to the new principal about what I was doing with consensus; I knew I had the superintendent's support but I felt concerned that the principal might not support it—might even stop the project before it had a chance to get off the ground. Because of my reticence, when the principal came into my classroom to evaluate my teaching, she had no idea of the intentions behind what she observed and made several criticisms that seemed harsh to me. I had attempted to arrange the desks in a big circle to facilitate egalitarian class discussions, but the size of the desks made it an awkward rectangle that skirted the room, and it was difficult to move around them. Her evaluation culminated in a written notice demanding that I come up with a new seating arrangement within a week.

At first I dug in my heels, certain that the principal had no right to tell me how the seats should be arranged in my classroom. I felt angry and powerless. However, when I stepped back to see a bigger picture, I realized that my larger goal of implementing the consensus classroom was more important than my immediate conflict with the principal. I also realized that I could continue implementing the consensus classroom while accepting her directive. I asked her if the students could participate in deciding how the seats would be arranged. She agreed, adding the stipulation that she wanted to see the plan before we actually moved the desks.

When I told my students, I wasn't surprised that they too were angry, and I found myself in the midst of teaching a spontaneous lesson about power struggles. I pointed out: "You often get into power struggles with each other or with adults in your lives, and some of you have gotten into them with me. Matt and I often get into power struggles, like the other day when he refused to do his math and had to stay in during break. We both ended up angry and feeling crummy about ourselves and each other." Though in a power struggle it may appear that there is a winner and a loser, actually both lose. In a power struggle between teacher and student, or principal and teacher, the one with greater authority often appears to be the winner; however, as in the example with Matt, the person in authority actually loses, too, because of hurt feelings and resentment.

After talking about power struggles and airing our feelings about the imperative, we were able to engage in a lively discussion about different room arrangements. We ended the period with an excellent plan for grouping in clusters, a plan that the principal approved and that the students could claim as their own, thus experiencing their authority and power as a group.

Consensus gave my students an alternative to power struggles. Students learned to listen to each other, to articulate their needs and wants, and to have their needs and wants included in the decisions. This provided them with a sense of their power to affect outcomes and removed the need to struggle. They learned to trust that issues were resolvable and that everyone could be a winner.

Avoiding Victimhood ❊ Power struggles often result in someone feeling like a victim. If something occurs that violates our sense of fairness or disturbs us in some other way–and we don't know how to affect change–we may fall into blaming others, looking to authority figures for rescue, or simply collapsing. We in effect give responsibility–and power–to someone else.

As my students learned to speak up for themselves and received feedback from each other, they sometimes discovered that others saw things in a similar way, which made them feel less alone. Sometimes other students were willing to change their behavior to accommodate the concern, which empowered the student who spoke up. Involvement in the consensus process helped students speak up for themselves in one-to-one relationships, as well as in groups. The listening and speaking skills we practiced in our consensus classroom contributed to our effectiveness in solving interpersonal problems. Students learned to express their concerns and needs without having to assign blame. Instead of "You shouldn't be doing that," they might say "This is how [naming the action] is affecting me."

> CONSENSUS GAVE MY STUDENTS AN ALTERNATIVE TO POWER STRUGGLES.

Through the consensus process, students also saw how their actions affected others in the group. When we discussed problems openly, we brought interconnections to light. My experience was that all children–even adolescents who might often appear mean–were really caring inside. When they knew that their own needs would be met and their own wants considered, they felt cared for and supported, and more open to considering the needs and wants of others.

At sixth grade camp one year, the students in one cabin group took an extra serving plate of desserts, so another cabin group did not get theirs. I was angry but baffled about what to do since the damage was already done–the dessert eaten– so I simply confronted the guilty group, pointing out that the other group missed out because of their action. A few minutes later, the offending group came to an excellent decision: "We'll give them our dessert tomorrow."

By listening to each other's needs, wants and feelings, my students could usually find solutions to their conflicts. The more experience they had with finding solutions that worked for everyone, the more faith they gained that problems were resolvable, without victims.

The inclusiveness inherent in the consensus process also encouraged diversity. Students experienced their power as equal to and shared with the others (power-with instead of power-over) reducing the sense of "winners and losers" or "us against them."

Enhanced Self-expression

According to common wisdom in the recovery movement, dysfunctional families enforce three unspoken rules to maintain the status quo: don't feel, don't trust, don't talk. In my experience, communication methods practiced in classrooms often reinforce these same dysfunctional rules. I believe involvement in the consensus process encouraged the opposites of these rules–do feel, do trust, do talk–thereby helping my students develop healthier relationships. Situations that encouraged speaking and feeling also encouraged trust–and vice versa. It took trust to feel comfortable talking about feelings, and the willingness to talk about feelings helped build trust.

Feelings Matter

Ignoring feelings can lead to poor decisions, as in the following personal story. A friend and I were hiking to the top of Yosemite Falls one sunny December afternoon. My boot slipped and I realized that the surface of the snow on the trail was getting icy in the cold afternoon wind. Earlier in the day I had read the caution to winter hikers that ankle injuries were a common preventable accident. As the sun started sinking, I became progressively more nervous about how long it would take us to hike back down in the slippery conditions and approaching darkness. My friend was having a grand time and did not want to acknowledge my fear. He decided (for both of us) that we just had to get all the way to the overlook. When I attempted to talk to him about turning back, he dismissed my fears and continued to hike. I then asked for the key to our car so that I could start back down the mountain alone. Part way down the trail I reflected upon what had just occurred. I realized that since he had not included it in the decision to hike on to the overlook, my fear became even stronger and led me into a foolish decision. I knew that separating was not a good idea (definitely not the best decision for both of us), but turning back alone seemed the only way I could take care of my fear.

> SITUATIONS THAT ENCOURAGED SPEAKING AND FEELING ALSO ENCOURAGED TRUST...

Unfortunately, in this culture we generally learn to ignore our feelings at a fairly early age. In my seven years of teaching sixth graders, I noticed that many of my students began the year with a sweet vulnerability, but gradually developed a tough shell, a callous insensitivity toward their feelings and the feelings of others as the year progressed. I remember that it was when I was in sixth grade that I first noticed my classmates "armouring" themselves around me. I was with three girl friends one day at a giant slide. Sliding down, I burned my arm against the edge of the slide. I nursed the painful wound for what must have seemed to my friend a long time, because she rolled her eyes and said, "Well, I guess we're not going to have any more fun today." I felt hurt and isolated, shocked into a painful awareness that I risked losing my friends' approval if I expressed my feelings around them. I think at that point I made a decision to suppress my true feelings in order to enjoy having their companionship.

Years later, as a middle school teacher, I felt myself armouring when on the playground or with the classes in which I was not yet practicing consensus. I felt compelled to enforce rules and consequences, distancing myself from the students and ignoring my feelings as well as theirs. In contrast, when my consensus students returned from break or electives and I shut the door to the rest of the middle school culture, I felt a sense of coming home–comfortable, supported and familiar. The consensus classroom became a sanctuary where it was okay to have one's feelings in the midst of a sometimes hostile middle school world.

As we practiced speaking up about how we felt, speaking honestly became a habit, like breathing. We learned to trust our own feelings and the feelings of others—even when they seemed to conflict with our own. We discovered that paying attention to feelings, and expressing them honestly and directly, eventually led to decisions that worked for everyone.

Speaking Up

For the first thirty-two years of my life, I was almost silent. I was a good student in school and had learned to sit still and be quiet, silently absorbing everything in my environment, internalizing it, processing it, and developing wisdom that I never expressed. My potential contribution was lost in my silence. Now that I have been participating in consensus decision-making for more than a decade, I find myself speaking up whenever I have an opinion. I speak up even when I don't feel strongly if I see that others want my opinion. In this case, I may only say, "Sounds good to me," or "I could go either way," but I do let my voice be heard.

My first involvement in the consensus process with the Audubon Expedition Institute two-year master's program taught me the importance of expressing myself. During the first year I held back, although I participated enough that my holding back was not apparent. I spent much of the time, as I had all my life, invisibly observing. I watched as the group heard and included the ideas and feelings of those who did speak up. I saw that at times we would come to an impasse and someone would point out that we were only hearing from a few people and we needed to hear more voices in the group. With more people's input, a better decision would become clear, or a creative new idea would emerge from one of the previously silent participants. I watched as some of the silent ones were challenged to speak up and saw how the group welcomed their perspectives. The second year, with a different group of people, I started speaking up regularly and participating more fully, which I have been doing in my life ever since.

My students learned through experience in consensus, that speaking up supported the consensus classroom in a number of specific ways:
- Contributing information that was needed, like missing puzzle pieces.
- Making connections between or among ideas.
- Offering creative new ideas.
- Asking clarifying questions (often a question that others had as well).
- Influencing the direction and focus of the conversation.
- Bringing attention to agreements that had been broken.
- Contributing intuitive insights.

- Bringing up problems or complaints that needed to be resolved so that the group could function more fully.
- Synthesizing ideas coming from different perspectives.
- Sharing feelings that revealed new dimensions of an issue.

In my consensus classroom, students got into the habit of speaking up, so they more easily resolved interpersonal conflicts on both an individual and group basis. And they often carried their communication skills onto the playground, into other classes, and into their lives at home.

During an interview for the video about the consensus classroom (Consensus Classroom, Inc. 2000), Rhonda demonstrated that she had gained the tools to effectively communicate feelings in her life outside the consensus classroom. She recounted an incident in eighth grade, when her teacher snapped at her and sent her out of the classroom. Later Rhonda spoke to the teacher about how she felt about the incident. The teacher not only listened to her, but–according to Rhonda–actually changed the way she treated other students as well.

Feeling Understood

It seemed to me that when my students trusted they would be "heard," they were more likely to speak up. I believe they wanted their perspectives to be understood even if others disagreed with them.

My students had different ways of responding when they felt misunderstood. Some would "shrivel." They stopped speaking at the least indication that listeners might not understand what they were saying. Others would repeat what they had said over and over.

Upon reflection, I noticed that when it was clear to me that I was understood, I felt validated and encouraged to expand my contribution–without feeling a need to repeat myself and without so much attachment to the decision going my way. What seemed important to me was that others understood what I was trying to say and took that perspective into consideration as part of the deliberations. I believe that when my students felt understood, they had more courage to bring forth their unique contributions. [1]

Love

When we welcomed and expressed feelings in my classroom, love often emerged. Students demonstrated amazing understanding and tolerance. One of my second grade students, a homeless child named Dora, carried a lot of anger

---

[1] *Active Listening* (Gordon, 1974) is a good way to help all members of the classroom have the affirmative experience of feeling understood. In Active Listening, the listener attends carefully to the speaker and then reflects back what he/she understands the message to be, as well as the feeling conveyed. The speaker can then clarify and/or amplify the intended meaning. In the process, the speaker usually feels heard and validated. Active Listening helps insure that everyone's feelings and thoughts are fully included in any decision made.

that she expressed in temper tantrums and by throwing things. I heard many complaints: "Dora hit me;" "Dora swore;" "Dora said I was stupid." She could have become an easy target to scapegoat and tease, but instead the opposite occurred. Just before winter break we planned a period to make mailboxes and put friendly notes in each other's boxes. The next day at class meeting, Dora expressed hurt feelings because she had only received one note. Others pointed out that they had only received one also. There had not been enough time for many of them to write. Later that day Dora received lots of notes. She kept coming up and showing them to me: "I like you, Dora." "Dora, you are nice." "You help me." The other students had taken her hurt feelings to heart and responded by giving her what she asked for, expressing their love without reservation, even though she had been mean to them many times.

> STUDENTS LEARNED THAT EVERYBODY'S VOICE MATTERED.

On another occasion in my second grade class, I set up a group collage-making activity. It turned out to be poorly planned. There were too many problems for me to handle, and too many students without enough direction. I was on edge, trying to help one student, when I looked up and saw Esteban push Stan. I let some of my built up frustration out on Esteban with an overly sharp reprimand. Later, I apologized to him. He forgave me easily and seemed to have let it go, but I had trouble forgiving myself. At the end of the day I still felt bad. My self-criticism was softened considerably when Jim, the last student out of the classroom, turned back and said, "I love you, Ms. Sartor."

Full Participation

Using the consensus process for decision-making promoted one hundred percent participation in my classroom. Students learned that everybody's voice mattered. And when everyone participated in the decision, the intrinsic motivation in each individual for supporting the decision increased, because participants had no reason to consciously or unconsciously sabotage the activity.

Full participation occurred within each student as well as within the group, creating a mutually reinforcing feedback loop (see p. 14). The energy generated was like a magnetic field that invited everyone in. As students were drawn into participation, they often uncovered new dimensions of themselves, and brought more of their full selves into the group activity. This further enhanced their motivation to participate fully in future decisions and activities.

Full participation occurred both in making the consensus decision, and in the activity itself. The degree of participation in the decision-making process was often reflected in the degree of participation in the activity. Even before I experienced the consensus process used extensively, I had found it useful to come to unanimous agreement in order to encourage full participation in P.E. "Before we go out," I would say, "I want everyone to agree about what we are going to do, because I want everyone to play." I had noticed that, without such agreement, some students would participate minimally or refuse to play altogether and sit on the side. Their lack of participation often disturbed the focus of the whole group. The activity was far more successful—and more fun—when everyone was fully involved.

Deciding on an activity by consensus generated enthusiasm for it and insured group focus. The particular activity chosen by consensus did not seem as important to the dynamic of full participation as the process of coming to a consensus about it. As the sole authority in the classroom—before I began using consensus as a general rule—I would "assign" a learning activity and then I would have to enforce rules and motivate the students with a reward/punishment system. I found it so much easier to maintain focus on an activity when the idea came from the students and they had agreed to do it. Students were generally more motivated to carry out decisions they had personally helped make.

> DECIDING ON AN ACTIVITY BY CONSENSUS GENERATED ENTHUSIASM FOR IT AND INSURED GROUP FOCUS.

One of my favorite illustrations of full participation occurred at the end of one consensus year. My sixth grade class went out to do a Yurt Circle, a group challenge activity in which everyone holds hands in a circle and individuals lean from their ankles, alternately in and out, counterbalancing each other (see p. 85). Each student ends up in a position impossible to maintain alone. While my class was involved in the Yurt Circle, a few stragglers who were not participating in their seventh grade P.E. class came over to interfere. Simply having seventh graders watching could be enough to distract most sixth graders, but my students were so involved that they ignored the other students, even when they began circling the group. I'm not sure whether any of my students even noticed. The magic of full participation was in effect.

I found that consensus leading to full participation was particularly easy with any activities that were generally recognized as "fun," such as physical education. I also experienced success with silent reading, literature, social studies, science, art, and even homework. With consensus my job was much easier because it awakened the intrinsic motivation of the students.

Silent reading was an activity that I could assign, but then I would have to act as "police person" to make sure everyone was participating. It worked better when the students suggested it and came to a consensus about it. Having experienced silent reading in earlier classes, they seemed to enjoy it because of the freedom to choose whatever they wanted to read and the relaxed atmosphere it provided. Every year someone would put it on the agenda as something to add to our day. When the idea for silent reading came from them and they all agreed to it, I could sit back and enjoy my own reading, modeling the behavior I wanted from them.

Choosing a literature book by consensus led to full participation in reading the book together. Once we all agreed on which book to read, interest in the content was enhanced and there were fewer complaints when it was time to read. Enthusiasm for and attention to the story was contagious, evoking the magic of being part of an active, focused group.

One year when we were studying Mesopotamia, the textbook suggested setting up a Mesopotamia fair in the classroom. I didn't feel strongly one way or the other about the activity, although I knew it would be valuable if everyone was interested in doing it, so I put the idea on the agenda for the next class meeting. We easily reached consensus in favor of creating the Fair. We then brainstormed potential topics and students signed up individually or in groups to create projects that demonstrated something about the topics.

We may have spent two periods–forty-five minutes each–of class time planning and starting the projects, and the rest was homework. Then we spent two more periods presenting the projects and giving feedback to each other. The tone was one of cooperative support. Everyone experienced teaching a brief lesson about his or her topic to the whole class. Through receiving and giving feedback, students practiced speaking honestly and sensitively in support of each other's work. My job was made easier by the shared responsibility, and the result was an impressive display that we saved for Open House.

I used a similar process with the science curriculum. At that time, our district didn't have a well-defined science curriculum, so individual teachers were free to come up with their own. This was an excellent opportunity for me to share this decision with my students and to take advantage of their interests, knowledge and resources as well as my own. First we brainstormed possible unit topics and chose one. Next we brainstormed questions and sub-topics. Each student signed up to research one of these sub-topics. While the students were doing research in the library, I had a welcome surprise. Because they had all been through the process of brainstorming topics as a group, each knew what everyone else was doing. While pursuing their own research, some students ran across something that they recognized would help someone else. I witnessed several whispered conversations in which students eagerly brought something useful to their classmates' attention.

> ...STUDENTS LEARNED HOW TO SPEAK HONESTLY AND SENSITIVELY IN SUPPORT OF EACH OTHER'S WORK.

The full participation generated in the consensus classroom enhanced my teaching of art. District guidelines did not require a certain amount of time for art, so it was up to me to decide how much to include. Teaching sixth grade, I found a great range in students' interest levels and attention spans for art activities. Some students seemed to think it was free time. Others whipped out something quickly and then were bored, sometimes troublesome, for the rest of the period. As a result I rarely set aside periods strictly for art, choosing instead to incorporate it into other learning activities.

However, I think art is a valuable activity in and of itself, so I was happy when students put it on the agenda. Then we planned art activities in which everyone participated eagerly, because they had all contributed their ideas and opinions and agreed on the projects. For example, one class decided on regular art periods with different students signing up to lead the activities. In the spring that year, a popular classmate taught us how to make paper bunnies. They were really cute and became a whimsical classroom decoration, even though it was the kind of project my students might have rejected as too childish if the idea had come from me.

Usually the first consensus decision I placed before my students on the first day of school was what to do for homework. When the class came to a consensus about homework, I got much better results than when I alone determined what the homework would be. For one thing, after an in-depth discussion about it, the students were more likely to remember that they had homework and what it was. Moreover, the reasons for doing a particular assignment usually came up in the course of the discussion, giving the students a better sense of purpose. Full participation in homework provided the huge benefit of extending the school day. When students complete work at home that otherwise would have to be undertaken during the school day, class time is freed up for consensus discussions and special class activities.

When everyone in a class had an investment in the success of their decisions, complex systems could develop that otherwise might not have worked. When implementing a money system in the classroom, for example, many small decisions needed to be made. The system was far too complex to be organized by a sole authority, but with shared authority the students made it work. We had to design a system that each person felt was fair. Whenever a problem arose—for instance, someone lost some money or someone began to mistrust the banker—we added it to the class meeting agenda and then came up with a solution that worked for everyone.

> IT WAS A JOY TO WORK WITH STUDENTS ...CARRYING OUT DECISIONS WHEN EVERYONE PARTICIPATED FULLY.

The money system developed in its own way each year. One year my students decided to pay themselves ten dollars of class currency each time they completed their homework, and to fine themselves twenty-five dollars when they did not do their homework. If I had come up with the idea, I think it would have seemed like punishment, because the fine was greater than the reward. Since it came from them, however, it worked to support them in doing their homework—much to my delight. Full participation was both a requirement for and a gift of consensus. It was a joy to work with students in making and carrying out decisions when everyone participated fully.

Creative Decision-Making

Along with shared authority, self-expression, and full participation, consensus decision-making promoted creativity. In my experience, majority rule decision-making tended to simplify issues to the limited perspective of either/or. In contrast, consensus tended to invite creativity from students as they explored the complexities of the issues involved. Individual perspectives—concerns, ideas, desires, skills, experiences, cultural influences—functioned as raw materials from which we created decisions. Moreover, consensus discussions often led to a deeper, more inclusive synthesis of ideas than that of which any one person could have conceived alone. Creative group thinking generated new processes, systems, activities, and ways to solve problems.

The court system and the money system—both developed through creative decision-making—also required creative decision-making in order to function. In one of the first court cases one year, a boy and girl were in conflict over a trivial issue and one of them brought it to court. After we heard all perspectives, the bailiff took the defendant and plaintiff out of the room while the rest of the class came to consensus about the verdict and sentence. I was impressed by the practical wisdom that emerged from the group in this case: that the boy and girl would have to sit next to each other. I appreciated the wisdom of this idea, because often under the surface, people in conflict are actually drawn to each other, and/or have something to learn from one another. Moreover, the "sentence" seemed to communicate a sense that the two students really needed to work out their conflict on their own, rather than taking class time for others to resolve it for them.

Just as consensus groups draw upon the resources and experience of individuals within the group, they may also draw upon creative decisions from previous years. The money system and the court system are both examples of ideas that developed from year to year. Because I relinquished control and allowed my students' creative ideas to develop, I witnessed an evolution of problem solving beyond anything I could have anticipated. Knowing I was part of the system—and that nothing could happen with which I was not comfortable—allowed me to trust that we could work problems out as they arose, although I did not always know exactly how. In short, consensus decision-making allowed me to get out of the way of the creativity of the group.

The consensus process gave rise to creative decision-making that included implementing new ideas and solving problems in new ways, and even creating complex systems that provided unique learning experiences.

Conscious Community

The consensus process helped develop the skills needed to create conscious community. My classroom community moved towards greater awareness of the dynamics beneath the surface of ordinary communication—dynamics such as individual wants and needs, gender and cultural differences, interpersonal conflicts, and power struggles. These dynamics affect everyone in a classroom, and if left unexamined, they may ensnare the group in unconscious patterns that hurt its members. Consensus encouraged individual students to speak up for their wants and needs, which often surfaced some of these underlying group dynamics. Then the class could own its collective responsibility for a given situation, and find creative solutions. Often, simply articulating the dynamics made the solutions obvious.

The development of conscious community through the consensus process served both individual members and the community as a whole in a mutually enhancing cycle. As the community became conscious of its underlying dynamics, and moved to self-correct any hurtful patterns, it became more welcoming and nurturing to its members, thereby enabling them to more fully bring forth their gifts. These gifts interacted together in a kind of alchemy in which new group capacities spontaneously emerged. Each conscious classroom community developed uniquely, a synergy of the individuals who comprised it.

Conscious Community Supports Its Members

Participation in my classroom communities accrued many benefits to my students and me, including:
- the experience of being seen, heard, and known
- a sense of belonging
- mutual care and support
- a direct experience of one's effect on others, and the effect of others on oneself
- the opportunity to make one's unique contribution
- a sense of personal power in affecting change
- the discovery of one's hidden agendas and unconscious behaviors
- the enlarging of one's resource base by pooling resources with others
- support for one's personal goals as part of a common vision

In one classroom community, Ann took Chris to court over a deal they had made using the class money system. Chris, who felt unpopular, became so anxious about the court case that she convinced herself that she was sick and asked to call home. When I suggested that her sickness might be due to the pending court case, she admitted that I was probably right. I pointed out that the longer she waited, the harder it was going to be to face, and she agreed to hold off on calling home until after court. I was a bit concerned about the outcome myself, but I trusted the process enough to know that whatever the outcome, she would have the opportunity to learn something valuable.

The results of the court case turned out far better for Chris than either of us had expected. The deal between Ann and Chris was found to be a "black market" deal, outside of the classroom money system agreements. Not only did the class agree that Ann had no right to sue Chris, they also decided that–since the deal was illegal–Chris no longer owed Ann anything. I imagine that Chris experienced a sense of belonging, and felt cared for and supported. Anne had the opportunity to glimpse the effects of her behavior on Chris and on the community as a whole.

This case validated the premise that children–all people, in fact–have a terrific sense of what is fair. I found that when given enough information, students could look beyond the surface dynamics of who they liked and disliked–or who was popular–in determining what was fair in a given situation.

Through his experience in the consensus classroom, Steve reaped many of the benefits mentioned in the list above. At the beginning of the sixth grade year, Steve frustrated the class because over and over again he would not agree when the rest of us were ready to come to consensus. During the course of the year, however, he found a unique way to contribute to the community by becoming "Dictionary Man." When we were reading out loud and we came to a word of which nobody knew the meaning, he would whip out his dictionary and look up the word for us. On the last day of school, Steve asked for time to give speeches because "I love this class," he said, and he wanted an opportunity to express that.

Pooling resources was a special gift to me as the teacher. Whenever we planned to do something together, students would discuss what was needed and who would bring it, so I no longer had to gather all the materials and resources myself. This was true for parties, projects, special events, crafts, and reward activities. This planning and pooling gave the students a sense of belonging and of contributing to the community. It was a way of expressing support and caring–and a relief to my budget.

> ...THE CONSENSUS PROCESS STRENGTHENED A SENSE OF BELONGING AND INCLUSION, WHILE DEVELOPING A SENSE OF PERSONAL RESPONSIBILITY.

In my sixth grade class each year, we all wrote individual goals and then developed a common vision that attempted to include all the individual goals. An example of a common vision was: "We support each other to do the best we can in the classroom and at school, to get good grades, get along with others and not get into trouble." The common vision was then posted in the classroom all year. Individuals were thus supported in realizing personal goals by a common vision that was held by all.

By its very nature, the consensus process strengthened a sense of belonging and inclusion, while developing a sense of personal responsibility. Because any decision that was not working could be changed and anyone could initiate the changes, every individual learned he or she could affect change in the community. In my classroom, anyone could add to the agenda at any time, any issue that occurred to him/her. And of course, everyone was included in the discussion and in making the best decision for the community at that time.

Consensus Practice Supports Conscious Community

The benefits that accrued to individual students through the consensus process enhanced their participation and strengthened the community as a whole. Members developed specific skills that further promoted conscious community, including:
- speaking one's truth clearly, directly, honestly
- listening for understanding with empathy
- holding an awareness of the whole
- giving and receiving feedback
- identifying and changing unconscious behaviors
- making and keeping agreements; confronting broken agreements
- acting spontaneously

Speaking One's Truth and Listening ❋ Developing speaking and listening skills was integral to the consensus classroom. Opportunities to practice these communication skills are not as available in classrooms where students are expected to sit still, be quiet, and follow instructions. As my students learned to speak up with questions, concerns, ideas and complaints, the classroom community became more responsive to the ever-changing wants, needs and potentials of that unique group.

Students in my consensus classroom also learned by experience how important it was to listen, because anything said might have direct bearing on their collective decisions. Everyone was affected by the decisions we made, so students experienced the consequences of not listening immediately. Moreover, when a student did not listen and said something that made this obvious, someone frustrated with this waste of time would usually point it out.

Awareness of the Whole ❋ When I made decisions as a teacher and sole authority, I could not know all of the concerns and issues involved. On the other hand, I found that the open, inclusive discussions of consensus enhanced everyone's awareness of the whole situation. My students and I heard multiple sides of any issue we addressed and a variety of concerns, as we worked together to make a decision that was best for us at that particular time.

> MY STUDENTS AND I HEARD MULTIPLE SIDES OF ANY ISSUE WE ADDRESSED, AND A VARIETY OF CONCERNS...

When I was the sole authority, the assumption seemed to be that there was one right way, one right decision, and as the authority, I knew it. In my consensus classroom, we all learned that no particular right decision existed in advance. Each class developed its own direction, based on the circumstances of each situation, which included the needs of the individuals involved and the welfare of the group as a whole. My classroom communities became more and more conscious as they discovered their own "right ways" through changing circumstances over time.

Feedback ❋ Mutual feedback among students and me helped build community. Throughout the year students practiced sharing their insights and experience directly, increasing the flow of information within the group. They learned to speak directly and effectively with anyone (including me) whose behavior disturbed them.

When my school district required that teachers nominate students in their classes for citizenship awards, I put the task on the agenda for consensus decision. I found this provided an excellent opportunity for feedback. Once we listed what made a good citizen in our classroom, students nominated other students, articulating how each met some of the criteria we had defined. Then we looked at the list of nominees and came to consensus about the suitability of each candidate. I was pleased to see that the students eliminated the names of those who commonly engaged in put-downs and name-calling, even if those students were "popular." The decision to exclude these students from citizenship awards helped them to become aware of their hurtful behaviors. Also through this process, some less visible students received supportive feedback about their unique contributions to the classroom community.

Identifying and Changing Behavior ❋ Through the feedback provided by their peers, students became more aware of the ways in which their actions and words affected others, so they could make conscious decisions about whether or not to change. At the beginning of one year, Ron nearly always disagreed when the rest of the class was ready to come to a consensus. As soon as a classmate pointed this out, Ron recognized what he was doing and changed; his disagreeing subsided. Another year, Danny really wanted to be our first banker, but other students said that they didn't trust him because he had let the class down several times by not keeping promises. He realized how important it was to the classroom community to follow through on what he said he would do, and he started acting more responsibly. Later that year he was elected banker.

> ...THE OPEN, INCLUSIVE DISCUSSIONS OF CONSENSUS ENHANCED EVERYONE'S AWARENESS OF THE WHOLE SITUATION.

In Ron and Danny's cases, simply naming the behavior pattern changed the dynamics. At other times, before any resolution could be reached, the class had to continue exploring thoughts and feelings in order to surface the underlying dynamics. When one class explored why Rachel felt the need to disagree so much, we uncovered her need for attention and a sense of power. The class found ways of meeting her needs that also supported the well being of the whole community; someone suggested she run for president in the next election.

Keeping Agreements ❋ Having participated in the process of making agreements, students were more likely to honor them. Each student had seen what was behind the decisions–the context, considerations, reasons, feelings, and other factors–and had a sense of ownership of them. Consequently, everyone had increased intrinsic motivation to keep agreements.

Students also developed the habit of reminding each other when agreements were not kept. Because everyone had ownership of these agreements, anyone could call attention to a broken one. Though many may have been uncomfortable about confronting each other at first, they became more comfortable with confronting broken agreements when it was an expected behavior in the culture of the classroom community.

Acting Spontaneously ❋ Once students in a given class learned to speak up if they disagreed with decisions made or actions being taken, the classroom community could behave more spontaneously. We would reach a level of trust in which anyone could make a suggestion and the group could move into action without needing to check for consensus. In this case, however, we <u>assumed</u> consensus, rather than making it explicit. Nevertheless, anyone could request that we check for agreement whenever he/she doubted that consensus had truly been reached.

Through developing and practicing consensus decision-making skills in the classroom, my students were empowered to speak up, to listen, to synthesize ideas, to have a sense for the whole community, and to recognize their own gifts—their wants, needs and feelings as well as their experiences, skills, abilities, and other resources—which contributed to the community. They not only felt included and important; they were! And they came to know that they could truly make a difference.

Through the process of creating a classroom community using consensus decision-making, I believe my students came to experience the unity beneath the surface appearance of separateness, and developed a strong sense of personal and social responsibility to their communities outside the classroom as well.

There are many ways to implement consensus in the classroom, and many possible outcomes. Here we have provided descriptions of systems and practices that proved successful for Linda and her classes. We encourage teachers (and their students) to pick and choose, combine and invent, in order to discover what works within their own situations. Once a system is in place, anything that proves unworkable to any individual—teacher or student—can be put on the agenda for reconsideration. Teachers can thus face uncertainty without needing to anticipate every possible problem in advance. Teachers and students alike enjoy more freedom to experiment, and to just be themselves.

CHAPTER 3

Community Building and Consensus: Practices from Linda's Classroom

Community Building and Consensus: Practices from Linda's Classroom

Consensus in the classroom is more than an instructional strategy or management system; it requires and creates a paradigm shift in a teacher's relationship with his or her students and in students' relationships with each other. The classroom becomes a lively learning community. Linda's stories about class meetings, interpersonal relations, a court system, a money system, decisions about homework, and a listening game bring to life her experience with this paradigm shift.

Whereas Chapter 2 discusses the general benefits and dynamics of consensus that emerged in Linda's classrooms, this chapter focuses on some of the specific practices that emerged. Again, we do not want these descriptions of Linda's experience to be seen as formulae, because we believe that each consensus classroom is unique and needs to develop in its own way. We include them here to stimulate thinking about what might work in other classrooms, what some of the possibilities might be.

Class Meetings[2]

Class meetings were essential to using consensus in my classroom. Students could depend on a regularly scheduled class meeting. A corner of the chalkboard was permanently allotted to "Class Meeting Agenda," which encouraged students to take action when ideas or problems arose. Beginning with the agenda, the consensus process encouraged everyone to participate.

Agenda

During the first class meeting each year, I wrote "Agenda" on the chalkboard and asked students to suggest items. We came to consensus about which items were a priority and discussed a few of them; then I copied the remaining items in a corner of the chalkboard for future meetings. Students could note new discussion items at any time on this on-going agenda. Election of class officers, interpersonal conflicts, new agreements, ideas for activities, changes in the way we did things, room arrangement, and personal complaints were among the types of

---

[2] Linda and her class certainly did not invent the idea of using class meetings as a structure for decision-making, which was a classroom management idea known to Linda from the beginning of her teacher training. Yet, the decision-making strategy in those other class meetings generally followed a model that included majority vote on the part of the students, with the teacher having veto power. The particular way Linda and her students implemented the general class-meeting strategy to support consensus decision-making was invented and developed by them over the seven years of time she used this strategy in her classes.

agenda items that students initiated. I initiated agenda items as well, to bring up my own concerns, to plan special events, and to fulfill school requirements such as student-of- the-month and citizenship awards. Any decision that was within my authority as the teacher in the classroom was a possible agenda item, but we could not make decisions that violated district policies or school rules.

I often began the process of creating the agenda for a class meeting by brainstorming with the students. Brainstorming is a way to create a list of possibilities–a very useful first step in many consensus decisions. When I introduced brainstorming to a class, I encouraged students to suggest whatever came to mind, with total freedom, even if some seem strange. We avoided evaluating or censoring any suggestions. To create an agenda, the class would brainstorm ideas, concerns, and problems that we might discuss during class meetings. From that list the class could select our first agenda.

> ...WE COULD NOT MAKE DECISIONS THAT VIOLATED DISTRICT POLICIES OR SCHOOL RULES.

Agenda items included–but were not limited to–topics that led to the following kinds of decisions: homework; a class reward activity; which literature book to read next; silent reading as a regular classroom activity; the P.E. activity for the day; rules to follow in a P.E. activity; how the class is to be managed (i.e. determining the expectations, consequences and incentives for the class assertive discipline program); development of a class court system; development of a class money system; the criteria for grading specific assignments; and implementation of student-taught lessons.

I set aside a regular time for class meetings, usually a half-hour a day just before lunch. Sometimes we did not resolve an issue by the end of the class meeting, so the item remained on the agenda and was carried over to another day. Someone might remove his/her item from the agenda before an actual decision was made–or even before discussion began–if it ceased to be an issue for that person. We would eventually discuss every item on the agenda until it was resolved, or removed by the person who placed it there.

Since each class meeting ended with the lunch bell, not everything on the agenda would get resolved. So we started each meeting by deciding what item was most important to discuss first. If there was still time when that discussion was complete, we would decide on the next item. Students learned to speak up for their concerns, and members of the class learned to listen carefully to one another in order to decide what should have the highest priority. Amazingly, it was quite often obvious to everyone which issue was most urgent, whether it was the concern of one person or the whole class.

One wonderful outcome of students having access to the agenda was that the ineffective dynamics of complaining disappeared. Whenever I overheard students complaining about something, I would suggest that they put it on the agenda, so that the problem could be confronted by all of us directly and changes could be made. Through practice, we all learned better both how to communicate and with whom, in order to effectively address our complaints.

Decision-making

Some consensus group facilitators feel it is important for each group member to speak before coming to a decision, so they systematically check in with everyone around the circle. I found that such a process was too time-consuming in my classroom, so when I modeled leadership of class meetings at the beginning of the year, I allowed discussion to last as long as anyone had anything to say, but I did not ask everyone to speak.

We would begin with an issue, idea, or proposal, as listed on the agenda. In some cases, simply having a discussion was enough to resolve an issue, even without coming to a formal decision. Perhaps people just needed to feel heard. For example, one day when there was a substitute teacher in the class, several students did not receive the Student Council "Candygrams" they had ordered. The substitute had set the candy out for them to take on an honor basis, and several disappeared. When I came back the next day, we focused on the problem for a full period without reaching a satisfactory resolution. The students' feelings of indignation and loss, however, seemed to dissipate simply from having everyone else consider and acknowledge the injustice. They erased the item from the agenda before the next class meeting.

When a proposal emerged and was articulated, it provided focus for the discussion. Anyone who had anything to say about the proposal had a chance to speak, and as a result the proposal would evolve. Sometimes, as part of the discussion prior to checking for consensus, I found it helpful to ask if there was anyone who disagreed. If so, the attention of the group could then go to that person's concerns and seek a way to modify the proposal in order to include those concerns. I would hold the discussion open until no one had anything more to say—no more questions, concerns or disagreements. I would repeat the final proposal as I understood it and write it on the board. Then I would say, "It looks to me like we might be ready to come to a consensus. Please get your hands up quickly and hold them up until we are able to look all the way around the room in order to make sure we're all in agreement."

> ...IT WAS QUITE OFTEN OBVIOUS TO EVERYONE WHICH ISSUE WAS MOST URGENT...

It would not necessarily have been an indication of consensus if I simply asked who didn't agree in the final poll, because someone might not have been paying attention, or might just be reluctant to speak up. Asking for a visible acknowledgement of agreement required all participants to make a deliberate indication of their commitment to the decision. Lack of action was an action because if someone failed to raise his/her hand, I would then ask why and we would continue the discussion as needed until that person was in agreement. I believe this deliberate indication of commitment evoked a greater sense of responsibility for the decision. Some people use a thumb approach for polling the group and/or checking for consensus. In this approach thumb up means "yes," thumb down means "no" and thumb to the side means "I don't know," "I have a question" or "I need further discussion." Another method, mentioned earlier, uses cards or slips of paper in three colors–green means "yes," red means "no," and yellow is "I don't know." This method did not work in my classroom the one year I tried it because some of my students had difficulty keeping track of their cards.

We found that it was always a good idea for someone to record our final decisions exactly as written on the board. We kept a file of our agreements so that we would remember them. I discovered that, after a discussion in which several different resolutions had been considered and refined, it was sometimes difficult to remember the final agreement precisely.

Leadership

I always began the school year leading the class meetings. However, each year in my middle school classroom, a student would usually place "election of class officers" on the agenda right away. When this item came up for consideration, we would write up job descriptions for the officers together. Class meeting leadership always became part of the job of the president and vice president.

Although some adults can successfully co-facilitate a consensus discussion, I found in my classrooms that consensus discussions worked best when only one person facilitated the meeting. Sometimes both the class president and vice president would place themselves in front of the classroom during a meeting, and the focus would break down when both of them started calling on different students at the same time or when the two of them got into separate conversations with different people. The rest of the class would not know to whom to listen and the discussion would deteriorate into several individual conversations. Whenever a meeting breaks down like this, people need to be reminded of the importance of listening to what each person has to say, because everyone's perspective is essential in coming to the best decision. This cannot be accomplished when more than one person is speaking at the same time.

Hand-raising

Occasionally we found that we could carry on a discussion without needing to raise hands to speak, but for the most part we found that several people would end up talking at once. So we needed to implement the usual classroom norm of raising one's hand and then waiting to be acknowledged by whomever was facilitating the discussion. Usually we had to establish some sort of system of consequences in order to support this process, because in the heat of a dynamic discussion it was difficult to remember to wait one's turn. At some point the leader might have to say, "OK, we need to start raising hands," and then impose previously agreed-upon consequences if necessary.

Majority Vote

One of my early classes created a new way of making certain types of consensus decisions that incorporated a majority vote. I found this method so useful that I suggested it to subsequent classes. We used it when we were deciding among a list of preferences generated through brainstorming. After the brainstorming, we would look over the whole list and discuss it. Anyone could eliminate an objectionable item. All the items on the final list had to be acceptable to everyone, although each person might have preferences among them. We then checked to make sure we were all in agreement to proceed to a vote on this list. Each person could vote for as many items as he or she wanted. The vote would reveal which item had the most interest. This voting-within-consensus method worked for decisions like P.E. activities, which literature book to read next, and what to do for homework.

Interpersonal Relationships

As I showed in Chapter 2, the use of consensus decision-making strategies helped improve communication skills and thus interpersonal relationships within my classroom. Several additional practices for further enhancing relationships evolved during this time.

The Disturbance Rule

At the beginning of each school year I had one primary class rule: stop doing anything that is distracting or disturbing to anyone else (my version of the Golden Rule). I have since heard someone refer to a similar rule as the Platinum Rule: "Do unto others as they would have you do unto them." For this "disturbance rule" to work, students had to assume responsibility for letting one another know when they were being disturbed. I found this expectation freed both me and my students, because when I had to be responsible for taking care of everyone's needs, I enforced a more rigid system of discipline than may have been necessary. When students were responsible for taking care of themselves, I needed only to take responsibility for myself and did not need to be monitoring what was happening on the other side of the room unless it was disturbing me.

> FOR THIS "DISTURBANCE RULE" TO WORK, STUDENTS HAD TO ASSUME RESPONSIBILITY FOR LETTING ONE ANOTHER KNOW WHEN THEY WERE BEING DISTURBED.

In speaking up for their wants and needs, students learn that different people have different tolerances. For example, Mary might be able to concentrate on her math assignment while Joe and Harry do a math drill out loud right next to her, but another student might be disturbed. Some people have different tolerances at different times. If Esteban is absorbed in his book during silent reading, he may not even notice Cindy talking to Katherine about what she is reading. On another day, however, Esteban's book may not be as interesting to him, so Cindy's talking would distract him.

Implementing the Rule ❋ The disturbance rule gave students a way to deal effectively with distracting movement, noise, put-downs, playful pushes, and other potentially annoying behaviors. I guided my students through the following steps:

1) Let the person know specifically what action is disturbing you.
2) If the disturbance continues, let me (the teacher) know. I can help clarify and reinforce the agreement.
3) If the disturbance still continues, let me know again, and I will follow through with the consequence that we have previously established.

Arguments and Tattling ❋ The disturbance rule also reduces the opportunity for arguments when the teacher, or anyone else, asks a student to stop doing something. For example, without the rule, students may protest, "But I was listening!" when asked to stop a side conversation during a lecture or teacher-led discussion. The reason for stopping the side conversation becomes the object of debate. However, with the disturbance rule in place, the teacher merely has to say, "Well, your side conversation is disturbing me," leaving nothing to argue about.

> THE DISTURBANCE RULE ALSO REDUCES THE OPPORTUNITY FOR ARGUMENTS ...

Students often "tattle" on one another, but when tattling is the norm, everyone is disempowered. Tattlers give up responsibility and power to the teacher, and the tattled-on have no chance to change their behavior without the intervention of somebody more powerful. The disturbance agreement can be used to transform "tattling" into "taking care of oneself" or "supporting another student." It is no longer possible to "tell on" someone just to get them into trouble.

For example, Larissa often told me when Joe wasn't following my directions. If it was a situation that was not creating a problem for me, I usually responded, "If that bothers you, let him know." Then Larissa had to decide if it was actually disturbing her and act accordingly. This reframed the whole situation and put both students in the best possible light. I didn't have to confront Larissa about her possible motivation (to get Joe into trouble) nor was I obliged to confront Joe.

When a teacher can reframe "tattling" as "support for another student," it can change the usual competitive dynamics that often exist in American classrooms. For example, Pedro pointed out to me that Elena had gum in her mouth. I responded loudly enough for Elena to hear, "Thank you, Pedro, for supporting Elena in following school rules. Elena, please get rid of the gum. Pedro, after this, you can just remind Elena yourself. You don't need to tell me. Then if she doesn't get rid of it and that disturbs you, you can let me know."

Instead of being reinforced in tattling and competition, Pedro learned another way of being in relationship with his peers—to support them in following school rules by talking directly with them. When my students reminded each other of school rules, rule-breakers had the opportunity to correct their mistakes and avoid teacher-enforced consequences. Moreover, I did not have to dish out consequences as often to ensure that students followed school rules.

In addition to tattling, students sometimes play another game when they look to an authority figure to take care of them; they try to make it appear that the teacher is playing "favorites." The disturbance agreement is an effective antidote to this game. For example, Tom is humming and I tell him that it is disturbing me.

"How come you don't say anything to Jill? She's humming, too," he challenges.

"I didn't notice Jill's humming, but I was disturbed by yours. If Jill is disturbing you, tell her, and you only need to let me know if it continues."

Whole Class Disturbance ❋ In my second grade class, I had developed a practice of calling for a minute of silence when the noise level began to get too high for me. I would count down from five to one and then everyone (including me) had to stay silent for one full minute. When verbal activity resumed, it was at a whisper level and the class usually remained calm for a while. After experiencing this enough times, some of the students themselves began to ask me to count down for a minute of silence when the noise level got too high for them. They had learned to effectively communicate their needs when something disturbed them, even if the disturbance arose from the whole class.

A Simple Conflict Resolution Process

At a group dynamics workshop for adults, I learned a simple communication process for conflict resolution. I have found the process to be effective for guiding people of any age through a conflict. It is a practice that is complimentary to consensus decision-making, because it encourages self-expression, listening, and self-responsibility, and recognizes the importance of all voices being included.

Each individual in the conflict has the opportunity to answer the following four questions uninterrupted:

1) What happened from your point of view?
2) How do you feel about it?
3) What do you want?
4) What are you willing to do?

Once each person has answered the four questions and heard the other's answers, the problem is usually resolved, but if not, there is a good foundation of information from which to build a mutually acceptable solution.

I found this to be a useful process on the playground when a student ran up to me with a problem involving another student. I also used it effectively with students working through a personal conflict during a class meeting.

Put-Downs and Name-Calling

Put-downs and name-calling frequently plague classrooms. Aside from creating a generally uncomfortable environment, these common behaviors undermine the sense of community that can develop in a consensus classroom. Students get caught up in a culture of put-down behaviors, both hurting others and being hurt themselves, sometimes without being aware of it. Timid students especially retreat further into their shells. Fortunately, the consensus process provides an excellent structure for confronting these hurtful behaviors.

Sometimes I was the one who initiated our first discussion about name-calling or put-downs, but oftentimes it would come from the students. Moreover, discussions described earlier about who deserved the school-wide citizenship awards provided an excellent opening for this topic. For student-of-the-month, we used a similar process to create a list of nominees, usually ending with a majority vote for our final selection of one student.

Some years the class even decided on consequences for students who engaged in put-downs. One year, students came up with the consequence of missing part of recess in order to write five good things about the person who was put down.

Court System

A court system evolved in several of my middle school consensus classes, providing a way to solve interpersonal conflicts. When the idea first came up on the agenda, I was afraid that a court system might lead to hurt feelings or become a vehicle for scapegoating. During the meeting, I raised these concerns with the whole class. They then became everyone's concerns and, since the students wanted the court system to work well, neither problem ever materialized. Actually, the court system proved to be quite a successful learning experience, as well as an effective strategy for group problem solving. Although each year it developed somewhat uniquely, I can describe how it typically worked.

> A COURT SYSTEM EVOLVED IN SEVERAL OF MY MIDDLE SCHOOL CONSENSUS CLASSES, PROVIDING A WAY TO SOLVE INTERPERSONAL CONFLICTS.

We elected a judge and an assistant judge, in case the judge was absent. During a trial, the classroom became the courtroom and the judge was in charge. We also elected a bailiff who swore the witnesses in. The jury was made up of the rest of the class, including the teacher.

When students had grievances that they wanted to take to court, they would write the names of the plaintiff and the defendant on the class meeting agenda. Court would usually take place at the next class meeting, as decided by consensus.

In the meantime, the defendant and plaintiff would each ask one classmate to represent them. During court, these "lawyers" would call up the witnesses, questioning and cross-examining them. Before making a decision, the members of the jury could also ask questions of the witnesses. When everyone in the room was clear about all aspects of the case, the bailiff would take the defendant and plaintiff outside the classroom while everyone else came to a consensus on the verdict and the sentence. The jury created unique (and often imaginative) sentences to match each case.

In the first year of the court system, the students wanted me to be the judge. Then they bombarded me with suggestions as to how I should conduct the courtroom. I had never served on a jury and they had watched a lot more TV than I had. I realized that they were more prepared than I for carrying out what they wanted, so I suggested that we elect a judge. The student judge acted more in accordance with their perceptions of how a courtroom should function, and I took my seat as part of the jury, with relief.

A Few Court Cases

Students demonstrated many times that they were fundamentally just and caring, as in the case mentioned earlier in which Ann brought Chris to court (page 34). Even though other students sometimes gave Chris a cold shoulder, the class/jury listened carefully to the case and came to consensus in Chris's favor. If it had been a popularity contest—which often occurs when we use the majority vote system—Ann might have won. However, by viewing the whole situation from each perspective, and then all of us consulting our own sense of justice, it became clear what was fair. Incidents like this alleviated my initial reservations about the court system.

> ... CONSULTING OUR OWN SENSE OF JUSTICE, IT BECAME CLEAR WHAT WAS FAIR.

By sharing authority through the court system, I didn't have to make decisions solely on the basis of my limited perspective, and students gained a greater feel for their own power and sense of justice. If I alone as the teacher authority had to decide what was best, I might not have had the time to get the full picture. The students affected by the situation and by my decision probably would not have seen the whole picture, either. In such a circumstance, students might have gone away feeling victimized and angry. In this case, Chris would have missed out on the opportunity to feel the support of her classmates, a rare experience for an unpopular student.

The court system provided lessons on so many levels that I could rarely predict where a given case would lead. One year, a student received a real-life lesson about civil disobedience and I received a lesson in the importance of speaking my truth. We had studied the civil disobedience of Martin Luther King, Jr. Moreover, my students knew that I had been arrested for protesting the testing of nuclear weapons. Angela decided to protest the sexism she perceived in the classroom because only boys had been elected to the offices of president and judge. She marched around the classroom with picket signs made of rulers and paper, and then posted them on the window. Even though other students told her that this behavior disturbed them, she continued over a couple of days. Several students became quite angry and took her to court.

The jury discussion regarding her sentence dragged on a long time. We considered and listed a number of consequences, including school detention, which I thought to be excessive. After much discussion, a student proposed a majority vote, which we sometimes used to choose from a list of preferences (as outlined earlier). All items on a majority vote list were supposed to be acceptable to everyone; unacceptable choices could be eliminated by anyone in the group.

I feared that if I eliminated the detention choice, the angry students would not be satisfied and the discussion would have to continue, taking up even more class time. Because I really didn't believe the majority of the class would vote for detention, I agreed to proceed to a vote. When the class indeed voted for detention, I was stuck with the onerous task of writing out a detention slip. I felt badly that Angela suffered a detention for her act of protest, although I realized that anyone choosing civil disobedience might suffer apparently excessive consequences. This was the lesson for Angela, while I learned a lesson about the consequences of going along with a decision when I really was not in agreement.

Money System

The first year I used consensus, in a sixth/seventh grade class, the students proposed the creation and use of class money. At first I resisted the idea, perceiving it as a system of extrinsic rewards. I was also reluctant to take on the bookkeeping and concerned about disagreements I foresaw. However, the students had so much desire to make it work, I was willing to try, knowing I could put on the agenda for further consideration any concerns that subsequently arose.

We figured out a management system employing an elected banker and assistant banker whom everyone could trust. They kept track of how much money each student earned and distributed the cash when needed. We decided by consensus how students would earn money, so I was not the sole authority to determine which behaviors to reward. Instead, the students decided what behaviors were important to them and used the money to support what they wanted to do anyway.

> ... THE STUDENTS DECIDED WHAT BEHAVIORS WERE IMPORTANT TO THEM ...

The class also decided by consensus how members could spend their money. We would have an auction at the end of each week, and anyone could bring in items to auction off. The shared responsibility for providing auction items meant I didn't have to buy trinkets out of my own pocket or from a limited classroom budget.

Since the bank continually paid out money as students earned it, and a relatively small amount was returned to the bank, we had to keep issuing more currency, creating an inflation problem. We partially curbed this inflation by requiring the sellers to give half of their earnings to the bank. One year I made the mistake of calling this a "tax." Later, when studying the origins of taxation in ancient Greece, my students' first thought was that taxes were created to stop inflation. So I stopped using the word "tax" in this context.

Another year, a black market developed to circumvent the fifty percent charge on auction sales: students started selling items to each other on the side. As previously mentioned, Ann tried to sue Chris in court over an agreement they had made in the black market, but as soon as we discovered that the case involved an illegal contract, we threw it out of court. This provided a real life lesson: if one operates outside the law, one doesn't receive the support of the law.

Commonly, some students would join together to pool their money, perhaps to increase their buying power in the auctions. At first, I feared this to be a set-up for conflict, but decided to trust that through the consensus process we could work out anything that emerged. The court system already established in the classroom handled some of the conflicts that arose that year, and any other problems were resolved without my intervention. Again, the learning that came out of the students' experiences went far beyond my formal lesson plans.

Each year the money system evolved a little differently, depending on the needs, wants, concerns and experiences of the individuals in the class. If the system didn't work, we changed it. During the first year, for example, the money system worked fine for a while. Then it stopped working after we connected it to the disturbance rule by requiring students to pay a dollar of class money to the person they disturbed. At least one student took advantage of this, telling others that they were disturbing him, just to get money. We stopped using the system not long after we had started it.

Since I was teaching a sixth/seventh grade combination class those years, several of the sixth grade students returned as seventh graders. When the idea of the money system came up again, the returning students and I resisted it because of our experience the previous year. Interest in developing a viable money system continued, however, so we examined what hadn't worked the year before. We then successfully created a new system. In subsequent years, I was far more positive about the whole idea, and even suggested it to some of my classes.

Each year in planning the money system, we had to make a number of decisions:

1. How do we earn money?
2. How much money do we earn for each activity?
3. What can money buy?
4. How much should things cost?
5. Who will design the currency?
6. How do we assure that the banker is someone everyone can trust?
7. How long is the banker's term of office?
8. How will we protect against counterfeit bills?
9. When and how will the cash be distributed?
10. How can we prevent inflation?

Answering these questions provided invaluable lessons in several social studies areas, and evoked much creativity from the class.

How We Did It One Year

A description of the fifth year that my class had a money system illustrates how it worked in practice. That year we had agreed to a classroom management system in which students' names were placed on the chalkboard for breaking class agreements. For repeated offenses, check marks were added next to names.

Students whose names were not on the chalkboard would be paid at the end of the day. My students also decided to be paid for doing their homework and to be fined when they didn't. Furthermore, they could earn money for staying to do the final clean-up in the classroom.

Money could be used in the weekly auction and to buy names and check marks off the board at the end of the day in order to avoid other consequences, such as seat moves and parent phone calls. It cost $25 to buy a name off the board. A check next to the name cost an additional $50 (a total of $75), and a second check cost an additional $100 (a total of $175). The third check cost another $200 ($375). This system gave both teacher and students more latitude in response to minor offenses. And the doubled cost of each succeeding offense assured that repeat offenders could only afford to buy their way out a few times before having to face more serious consequences.

> THIS SYSTEM GAVE BOTH TEACHER AND STUDENTS MORE LATITUDE IN RESPONSE TO MINOR OFFENSES.

As we set up the system that fifth year, Danny volunteered to design our currency, although we had to wait for him to follow through before the system could start. Other years there were a number of students who wanted to design bills, so we agreed to make it a contest, deciding which bills by majority vote. At first I had to initial every bill in order to avoid counterfeiting, but then we came up with the idea of printing the bills on green paper so they couldn't be copied without clouding.

The banker and assistant banker, who served a two-month term of office, were elected from a group of nominees whom everyone agreed they could trust. Once the list of nominees was on the board, anyone could say why he or she didn't trust one of the people on the list, and that name would be eliminated that month. For example, as described earlier, Danny's delay in designing the currency and his absentmindedness about other promises to the class led to concerns from several of us when he was nominated banker that first term, so we removed his name from the list of nominees at that time.

That year, students were paid each morning for homework, and at the end of the day for other reasons. Other years the banker would keep track of earnings for the week, and payment was made on Fridays before the auction.

We set up checking accounts that fifth year because some students were intrigued with the idea, but the use of checks proved to be more cumbersome than beneficial. No one used them after the initial excitement, so checking accounts died out. In another interesting development, a group of students who had been saving their money opened a loan company for other students who had depleted their funds through paying fines.

Decisions about Homework

As I mentioned earlier, I introduced consensus on the first day of school by guiding my students to a consensus about their homework that night (see p. 32

for more details.) After that, what to do for homework became a daily decision. District policy dictated that sixth and seventh grade students be assigned an hour to an hour and a half of homework each weeknight, so the class could not opt out of homework altogether. I told them of the district guidelines—the time requirement and that homework was to be an enhancement and practice of the learning that was taking place in the classroom—and the discussion went from there, leading to our first consensus decision.

The next day, we brainstormed some of the criteria that could be used to evaluate the homework assigned the day before, and possible attributes of better-than-average work. I then had the students share their homework in small groups for feedback. They graded themselves (with C+ being average) based on the feedback that they received in their small groups. They turned their homework in with their suggested grades and reasons for the grades. Based primarily on the reasons given by the student, I agreed or disagreed with each grade, and explained my decision in my response to the student. I thought that this process—sharing their homework with their classmates and evaluating themselves—encouraged them to take pride in their work. It also took the burden of evaluation off me, at least in this one area.

The practice of students making the decision about what to do for homework each night led to some wonderful unexpected outcomes. In addition to the ownership they felt and their increased understanding of the rationale of the homework assignments, a third benefit emerged. When we wanted to use class time for an important activity that we had chosen together, we could make time in the schedule by taking work home that otherwise would have been completed in class. When students consistently did their homework, it actually served to extend our class day by an hour or so.

Some time into the year, it became difficult for the class to think up interesting homework, so the students welcomed the science fair and other school-wide events that provided projects for stimulating new homework assignments. The students participated much more enthusiastically in those events than I had previously experienced.

For their first homework assignment one year, my students decided to design and make a paper airplane, and then write up the instructions to enable someone else to reproduce it. This assignment created high interest and took most of them more than the required hour and a half to complete. It also tapped into a wide variety of skills, including articulating and following directions. The next morning the classroom was quite a scene. Each student received another student's instructions and attempted to construct that airplane. Soon there were paper airplanes flying all over the classroom.

> STUDENTS...ARE MOTIVATED TO LISTEN WHEN THE CLASS DISCUSSES DECISIONS THAT WILL DIRECTLY AFFECT THEM.

Homework assignments that my students chose included: creative writing combined with artwork, free reading with some sort of creative response to the reading, extra math practice (problems at the back of the book), science projects, activities that provided extra practice with spelling words, and watching and reporting on an educational TV show or the news.

The Listening Game

Students naturally tend to listen well as part of the consensus process; they are motivated to listen when the class discusses decisions that will directly affect them. However, I found that the same students who avidly listened during class meetings often did not pay close attention to morning announcements. After a little reflection, I realized that the announcements were often about something that was not yet "real" to the students. When it did become "real" later, I would have to answer the same questions over and over again, which frustrated me. So I created the Listening Game to give students more motivation to listen to announcements. After trying it out a few times, I realized that the game was applicable to other situations as well.

I would devise a ten-point quiz that I gave immediately following announcements (or whatever material I wanted the students to hear). If 70% of the class scored 70% or better, the class received a point (ten points earned a class-planned period). Students were not allowed to help each other during the quiz. Immediately after collecting the quizzes, I reviewed the correct answers out loud. Now, the students had more of a reason to listen for the answers—in order to determine how well they had just done. This game actually gave the students three opportunities to think about the information: when I first made the announcement, when the question was asked in the quiz, and when the answer was given after the quiz was collected. I think that one of the reasons that the Listening Game worked so well was that there were no negative consequences attached—there was nothing to lose. Everyone was a winner just from playing the game, and the class worked together to earn the reward.

For the first quiz, I would devise questions checking for understanding of the rules of the game. Here are some true/false examples: 1) It is okay to help each other on this quiz (F); 2) I can use my notes when taking this quiz (T); 3) Seventy percent of the class needs to get at least seven questions correct in order to earn a point toward a class-planned period (T); 4) If I do poorly on this quiz it will affect my report card grade (F).

I played the Listening Game whenever I wanted to encourage attentive listening—for example, when I read Greek myths out loud to the class. I found this activity especially useful when students presented projects or stories orally to each other. The game motivated students to listen carefully to each other's presentations. Furthermore, students received practice in the listening skill of note taking when I allowed them to use their notes during the quiz.

There are many ways to implement consensus in the classroom, and many possible outcomes. Here we have provided descriptions of systems and practices that proved successful for Linda and her classes. We encourage teachers (and their students) to pick and choose, combine and invent, in order to discover what works within their own situations. Once a system is in place, anything that proves unworkable to any individual–teacher or student–can be put on the agenda for reconsideration. Teachers can thus face uncertainty without needing to anticipate every possible problem in advance. Teachers and students alike enjoy more freedom to experiment, and to just be themselves.

As a way to implement progressive, humanistic and holistic ideas, consensus decision-making helps build collaborative learning communities, and empowers students to take responsibility for decisions affecting their ever-changing world.

The post-modern paradigm calls for an altered sense of authority for both teachers and students and a more democratic social structure in the classroom, one that provides greater opportunities for individuals to make choices in harmony with community needs.

CHAPTER 4

Consensus in Post-Modern Education

Consensus in Post-Modern Education

Many educators today find themselves in the midst of a profound paradigm shift that parallels the larger cultural shift into a post-modern world. As William Doll (1993) and William Berquist (1993) both observe, the term "post-modernism" is difficult to define, and means different things to different people. In our understanding, it refers to the paradigm shift in which much of the developed Western world is currently immersed—so deeply that many of us find it difficult to gain sufficient perspective to be able to define it. Key to this shift is a move away from the "modern" view of reality as linear, uniform, measured, and determined, and toward a sense of reality as emergent, contextual, and co-created through interaction. In a sense, post-modernism could be understood as a label given to the state of unpredictability and complexity that we are coming to realize is the condition within which all life exists and functions. This can be a frightening realization to people conditioned to believe that, through scientific knowledge, we humans can understand and control our world. In a post-modern view, life is always in transition—always in a state of uncertainty, ambiguity, and paradox.

In this chapter, we explore some of the central challenges of the post-modern paradigm that have surfaced in educational literature. Educational theorists since the time of John Dewey have contributed to this shift, through progressive, humanistic, and holistic concepts. In the last few decades, cooperative learning and environmental education have provided practical methods for putting the new paradigm thinking into action. Consensus in the classroom can provide further support to these various approaches in meeting the challenges of education in the twenty-first century. As a way to implement progressive, humanistic and holistic ideas, consensus decision-making helps build collaborative learning communities, and empowers students to take responsibility for decisions affecting their ever-changing world.

The post-modern paradigm calls for an altered sense of authority for both teachers and students and a more democratic social structure in the classroom, one that provides greater opportunities for individuals to make choices in harmony with community needs. New understandings about thinking and learning processes call for more emphasis on inquiry, experiential learning, the questioning of assumptions, the blending of action and reflection, and seeking the synthesis of apparent polarities and conflicts. Educators have discovered the power of cooperative learning communities that engender self-responsibility and self-direction within their members, while seeking decisions that enhance the health and welfare of the whole community. The post-modern paradigm calls for the celebration of diversity, and the inclusion of all voices in the conversation. Communication skills and practices are perceived as central to learning and to healthy classroom functioning. Ultimately, post-modern education calls for learning to be relevant to life both inside and outside the classroom, enabling students and teachers alike to meet the enormous social and environmental crises of our time.

Authority, Democracy, and Individual Choice

As the father of progressive education, John Dewey would probably jump for joy if he could see consensus at work in a classroom. Though his work established a solid philosophy of education, he himself acknowledged that his principles alone did not solve the problems of the practical conduct of progressive schools. The consensus process directly addresses many of the problems he illuminated.

Dewey (1938) criticized both "traditional education [which] entailed rigid regimentation and discipline that ignored the capacities and interests of child nature," and the reaction to traditional education, which fostered "inchoate curriculum and excessive individualism." He advocated an educational approach more in accord with democratic ideals than the autocratic procedures of traditional schools. He believed (and many educators today agree) that democratic social arrangements promote a higher quality of human experience for more people than do methods of repression, coercion, or force. Consensus provides a structure for a democratic social arrangement in the purest sense–government by the people. While engaged in the consensus process in the classroom, the teacher can function in the way Dewey hoped: "can exercise the wisdom of his[/her] own wider experience without imposing a merely external control" (p. 38).

> ... THERE IS AN INTIMATE AND NECESSARY RELATION BETWEEN THE PROCESSES OF ACTUAL EXPERIENCE AND EDUCATION.

Authority

Dewey (1938) identified the basic conflict in education theory–between development from within the learner and formation imposed upon the learner from the outside. He believed that the source of knowing is within the individual learner and "there is an intimate and necessary relation between the processes of actual experience and education" (p. 20). The "importance of the participation of the learner in the formation of the purposes which direct his[/her] activities in the learning process" was primary to his concept of progressive education. As we illustrate in this book, consensus in the classroom can involve the learner in both defining the purposes of learning activities and selecting the activities that best serve those purposes. The authority for learning then resides in the learner in collaboration with the teacher, rather than in the teacher-as-expert alone.

Other educational theorists express similar concerns about authority in the learning process. Alfie Kohn (1993) remarks, "A teacher that makes unilateral decisions, regardless of their merit, is in effect saying that the classroom does not belong to the students but only to her[/him]; their preferences do not matter. People do not usually cheer when things are done to them. That is why teachers contemplating a new way of doing things ought to bring the children in on the process" (p. 199).

Edward Cell (1984) describes what he calls "response learning" as a rudimentary form of education in which an outside authority determines what is best for his/her students, rewarding them when they are performing according to the standard, and punishing them when they are not. Jack Mezirow (1991) would describe this sort of learning as "mindlessness" which "leads to self-induced dependence on external authority, diminished self-image, and reduced growth potential" (p. 115). Cell describes dysfunctional or "de-centered" learning as adopting the behavior and beliefs expected of us by others, and contrasts it with "centered" learning which is deriving our beliefs from our own experience. He concludes that a strategy of meaningful survival would include: 1) knowing oneself well enough to stay self-oriented; and 2) knowing how to get one's contributions to the organization seen and valued. Learners engaged in a consensus decision-making process are called to develop and practice both these capacities.

Paulo Freire (1997) decries "the 'banking' concept of education" which mirrors Cell's "response learning" and Mezirow's "mindlessness." "In the banking concept of education" the scope of action allowed to the students extends only as far as receiving, filing, and storing the deposits [made by the teachers]" (p. 53). "The more completely students accept the passive role imposed on them, the more they tend simply to adapt to the world as it is and to the fragmented view of reality deposited in them" (p. 54). The banking system of education thus serves to keep the systems of domination in place. The adapted person is honored as "the educated individual," because she or he is better "fit" for the world. "Translated into practice, this concept is well suited to the purposes of the oppressors, whose tranquility rests on how well people fit the world the oppressors have created, and how little they question it" (p. 57).

> ... THEY TEND SIMPLY TO ADAPT TO THE WORLD AS IT IS AND TO THE FRAGMENTED VIEW OF REALITY DEPOSITED IN THEM.

"There is no such thing as a neutral educational process," concludes Freire (p. 16). An educational process either functions to bring about conformity to the system or to bring about the discovery of how to participate in the transformation of the world. Freire sees true education as a process of inquiry such that "[both teacher and students] are simultaneously teachers and students" (p. 53).

Parker Palmer (1998) writes: "...we often confuse authority with power, but the two are not the same. Power works from the outside in, but authority works from the inside out.... Authority is granted to people who are perceived as authoring their own words, their own actions, their own lives, rather than playing a scripted role at great remove from their own hearts" (pp. 32-33).

"To educate is to guide students on an inner journey toward more truthful ways of seeing and being in the world," says Palmer (p. 6). "[Our teachers'] power is in their capacity to awaken a truth within us" (p. 21). "The kind of teaching that transforms people does not happen if the student's inward teacher is ignored"

(p. 31). Palmer admits, however, that operating on these beliefs offers a significant challenge: "I must learn how to trust that the community has the resources necessary to deal with the issue at hand" (p. 134).

Ruth Charney (1991) stresses the importance of the teacher seeing his/her own authority within:

> ... Authenticity is not about getting children to love or obey us, or even to admire our talents. Authenticity is about knowing oneself well enough to allow others to know themselves....

Authentic teaching requires and encourages personal authority. This authority is not so much an office as it is a way of acting. We stake a claim–in the classroom and in the larger context of schools and systems–to what is personally, intimately known and felt. Personal authority means that perceptions and values are not easily repudiated or pushed aside because others–even those with official authority–disagree. Disagreements may spark investigation and spirited discussions, but they can't force denial of our thoughts and principles. Authenticity involves accepting our personal authority–and the risks that go with it–so that we can be agents of the changes needed in our schools (p. 259).

Democracy

Democracy is also a common theme permeating new paradigm thinking in education. As cooperative learning educator Spencer Kagan (1994) inquires:

> How can we possibly prepare our students for full participation in a democracy by structuring our classroom autocratically? It is an amazing feature of our democratic educational system that we have settled so universally on an autocratic social organization of our classrooms. The teacher is the Congress (making the laws), the President (carrying them out), as well as the Judge, the Jury, and too often, the Executioner. Is it any wonder that teachers feel tired at the end of the day? (p. 9.1)

Democracy–government by the people–has been implemented in the USA through a majority vote system. Some holistic educators call for something beyond majority vote in educating for democracy. Phil Gang (1989, p. 46) discusses how we are moving "out of the age of making decisions based on 'either-or' alternatives." He suggests that we need to recognize "the possibility that a multitude of solutions may exist, each one equally as plausible as the next." One of the goals for democratic education articulated by Gang is: "...to help students understand that a variety of solutions may be valid in any particular circumstance." Decision-making by consensus provides a form of democracy in which decisions are not reduced to "either-or" and multiple alternatives can be explored and synthesized.

"The principles of a democratic society have to be 'lived' in the classroom if students are going to understand the full impact of their meaning. You cannot teach democracy through non-democratic methods," asserts Gang (p. 52). "Participation enables youth to acquire control and to internalize the experience of effecting events." He concludes, "as adults these individuals become aware of their faculty to bring about change. They are active rather than passive." Participation in a consensus classroom provides students with daily experience in their capacity to bring about change, thus developing both the skills and attitudes necessary for effective democracy, in and outside the classroom.

Choice

Central to concerns about democracy and authority in education is the question of choice. Who gets to choose what and how the student should learn? William Glasser (1998) found that only about 25% of the students in high achieving schools, and 5% in many large inner-city schools, actually make an effort to do what they are capable of doing in school. He believes that a significant factor that contributes to these low figures is teachers imposing "learning" on their students through force and punishment.

> The main reason so many students are doing badly and even good students are not doing their best is that our schools, firmly supported by school boards, politicians, and parents, all of whom follow external control psychology, adhere rigidly to the idea that what is taught in school is right and that students who won't learn it should be punished. This destructive, false belief is best called schooling.... Forcing people to learn has never been successful, yet we continue to do it because we think it is right. (p. 237)

Ruth Charney (1991) conveys a similar perspective: "Children are growing up in a world with frightful persuasions and terrifying problems. Rather than providing prescriptions for them, we need to make choices and decision-making part of the expected curriculum" (p. 190).

Many teachers seeing the disadvantage of managing their classrooms through punishment have tried switching to rewards. This shift does serve to support a more positive atmosphere in the classroom, yet a rewards system is still teaching students that there is an external authority who knows what is right. Moreover, some teachers have found that students who have been influenced by reward systems lose their sense of internal motivation; "What do I get if I do it?" has replaced, "What happens if I don't?" Alfie Kohn (1993) cites research showing that teachers are discovering that rewards are not effective, and he too supports the idea of choice:

> A recent national survey of elementary school teachers found fairly widespread understanding that rewards are not particularly effective at getting or keeping students motivated. Such strategies as awarding special privileges to those who do well were seen as less successful than giving students more choice about how to learn or letting them work together. (p. 226)

Kohn identifies three components of effective motivation—collaboration, engaging content, and choice. He suggests the question of how to motivate is not even appropriate to ask, because children are hungry to learn—to make sense of their world. "Given an environment in which they don't feel controlled and in which they are encouraged to think about what they are doing (rather than how well they are doing it), students of any age will generally exhibit an abundance of motivation and a healthy appetite for challenge" (p. 199). "A child who can make choices about what happens in his or her classroom is a child who will be less likely to require artificial inducements to learn and more likely to get hooked on learning" (p. 221).

Kohn specifies three reasons for giving children choice: 1) it is intrinsically desirable because it is a more respectful way of relating; 2) it offers benefits for teachers such as making the curriculum more interesting to them and freeing them of the chore of constantly monitoring and supervising; and 3) it works better. He cites a number of studies that have shown that choice works better. Here is a sample of the results of these studies:

> When teachers of inner city black children were trained in a program designed to promote a sense of self-determination, the children in these classes missed less school and scored better on a national test of basic skills than those in conventional classrooms. Fourth-, fifth-, and sixth-grade students who felt they were given personal responsibility for their studies had 'significantly higher self-esteem and perceived academic competence' than children who felt controlled in their classroom. The evidence goes on and on. At least one study has found that children given more "opportunity to participate in decisions about schoolwork" score higher on standardized tests. They are more likely than those deprived of autonomy to continue working even on relatively uninteresting tasks. They are apt to select assignments of the ideal difficulty level so they will be properly challenged (assuming there are no rewards involved). (pp. 222-223)

Kohn emphasizes that he is not talking about perfunctory choices "like which of three essay questions they will address," but rather "about giving students of all ages considerable discretion about things that matter in the classroom" (p. 223). He points out that there are many different ways to implement student self-determination depending on "the age of the students, constraints placed on the teacher, and the teacher's need for control, among other factors" (p. 224). Consensus in the classroom provides teachers with an excellent system for implementing student self-determination, within the constraints of the situation and the teacher's gradually expanding comfort zone.

New Pedagogical Understandings and Challenges

New understandings about the learning process–how the brain processes and integrates information and the different kinds of intelligence–influence post-modern educational theory and practices. Experiential learning, the necessity of questioning unconscious assumptions, inquiry, and cycles of action and reflection are among the pedagogical approaches that are being explored in classrooms. Consensus decision-making can play a key role in implementing any and all of these approaches.

Again we can look back to John Dewey (1938), who based his progressive education on experience, experiment, purposeful learning, and freedom. According to Dewey, "learning in the way of formation of enduring attitudes may be and often is much more important than the spelling lesson or lesson in geography or history that is learned. For these attitudes are fundamentally what count in the future" (p. 48). He saw the desire to go on learning as the most important attitude that a student could develop. Classroom consensus decision-making builds on and supports each student's natural desire to learn.

Brain Research

Renate Nummela Caine and Geoffrey Caine (1994) show that many state-mandated texts and curricular requirements are at odds with the latest research on how the brain works. They conclude, "...educators, by being too specific about facts to be remembered and outcomes to be produced, may inhibit students' genuine understanding and transfer of learning" (p. vii). Coming to terms with complexity, tolerating ambiguity, and accepting active uncertainty are critical. "Brain research establishes and confirms that multiple complex and concrete experiences are essential for meaningful learning and teaching" (p. 5). If we teach in accordance with this research, we may see "the emergence of learners who can demonstrate a high level of basic competence, as well as deal with complexity and change" (p. 7).

The Caines (p. 85) indicate five conditions that "increase the brain's capacity to function in complex ways and create new connections." Three of these conditions are well supported by the use of consensus in the classroom: 1) outcomes should be relatively open ended; 2) personal meaning should be maximized; and 3) emphasis should be on intrinsic motivation which is fostered when people have a sense of ownership in the process. The Caines call for teachers to develop an approach that combines planning with opportunity for spontaneity–by both teacher and students (p. 117). "What is needed," according to the Caines, "is a framework for a more complex form of learning that makes it possible for us to organize and make sense of what we already know" (p. viii). Consensus decision-making contributes to such a framework when used consistently in a classroom, developing everyone's capacity to tolerate ambiguity and deal with complexity and change.

> WHAT IS NEEDED ... IS A FRAMEWORK FOR A MORE COMPLEX FORM OF LEARNING THAT MAKES IT POSSIBLE FOR US TO ORGANIZE AND MAKE SENSE OF WHAT WE ALREADY KNOW.

Inquiry, Action, and Reflection

Many educators today encourage inquiry as a primary process for learning, often in cycles of action and reflection. Freire (1997) suggests the idea of "praxis"–action and reflection upon the world in order to change it. Freire assumes: 1) that the world is not a static given reality, and 2) that humans act upon and transform their world, which in turn moves them toward new possibilities for a fuller and richer life. He calls for teachers and students to attain knowledge through common reflection and action and thus discover themselves as their reality's "permanent re-creator." He suggests that "people teach each other, mediated by the world.... The students—no longer docile listeners—are now critical co-investigators in dialogue with the teacher" (pp. 61-62). Consensus decision-making shines as a powerful method of implementing "praxis."

Similarly, Jack Mezirow (1991) explores how students can reflectively assess the premises behind meanings, purposes, and values—instead of passively accepting social realities defined by others. He sees transformative learning as emancipation from assumptions that limit our options and choices—assumptions that have been taken for granted or seen as beyond human control. In the consensus classroom, we frequently are required to surface our underlying assumptions, in order to reach consensus. Sometimes, we are operating on an assumption that no longer serves us. Articulating our own assumptions and hearing those of others makes these more conscious and thus more readily examined. Surfacing and examining assumptions leads to changing some that have become obsolete and expanding to include more—following Mezirow's vision of transformative learning.

In his principles for effective teaching, Stephen Brookfield (1986) calls for a continual process of activity and reflection upon that activity, which is similar to Freire's praxis. Like Mezirow, Brookfield also calls for critical reflection on values, beliefs, behaviors, and ideologies, recognizing these as culturally transmitted and thus provisional and relative. Consensus decision-making requires constant reflection on values, beliefs, behaviors, and ideologies, while discussing alternative choices and their probable consequences. Through participating in the consensus process, students experience the validity of a variety of perspectives.

A Paradigm Shift for Curriculum

Taking into account all the shifts in authority, democracy, and choice, and the attendant pedagogical challenges that we have surfaced so far in this chapter, we now consider curriculum. William Doll (1993) writes of the opportunities inherent in the challanges educators face:

> The loss of certainty encourages if it does not cause us to dialogue and communicate with others... Our sense of self and reality as independent objects is meaningless. We are able to discern ourselves only in terms of others, reality only in terms of imaginations. Both self and reality are found in relations... . (pp. 61-62)

> ... Utilizing disparate trends—paradoxes, anomalies, indeterminacies—is one of the greatest hurdles traditional educators and curricularists have in accepting an eclectic and diverse post-modern pedagogical frame. If such acceptance can be accomplished, though, the pedagogic possibilities inherent in a post-modern frame are unlimited and immensely exciting, for both teachers and students. (p. 128)

Doll believes that in post-modern times, we need to encourage abilities such as "purposiveness," self-organization, and communication in our students through our curriculum. He suggests that the teacher's art is to help disequilibrium to occur and then also to constrain the disequilibrium such that it does not turn into "unbridled disruption" (p. 83). The use of consensus decision-making strategies in the classroom does just that, because the teacher does not have control over the thoughts, feelings, and experiences the students bring, nor the issues that will arise. Yet, because he/she is part of the consensus, the teacher is able to maintain a sense of control, or what we might call "bridled disequilibrium."

A curriculum that responds to the needs of post-modern times may have more complexity than traditional curricula. Doll describes this complexity as a creative force that contributes to transformation:

> The linear, sequential, easily quantifiable ordering system dominating education today—one focusing on clear beginnings and definite endings—could give way to a more complex, pluralistic, unpredictable system or network. Such a complex network will, like life itself, always be in transition, in process. A network in process is a transformative network, continually emerging—one moving beyond stability to tap the creative powers inherent in instability. In such a transformative network, prediction and control, key elements within the modernist curriculum model, become less 'ordered' and more 'fuzzy.' Really what happens is that a whole new sense of order emerges: not the symmetrical, simple, sequential order classical science borrowed from medieval thought, but an asymmetrical, chaotic, fractal order we are now beginning to discover in the post-modern sciences. (Doll, pp. 3-4)

What Doll describes is much like the experience of participating in a consensus classroom. "The art of curriculum construction," according to Doll, "is that of helping students develop their own creative and organizing powers" (p. 117). He concludes that "curriculum is not just a vehicle for transmitting knowledge, but is a vehicle for creating and re-creating ourselves and our culture" (p. 131). Thus "curriculum—as a total package with content and instruction entwined—becomes exciting and engaging as it spirals off into the unknown" (p. 102). The process of consensus decision-making also "entwines" content and instruction, as students grapple together with the "content" of the issues addressed, as well as the process of decision-making itself. As a classroom begins to function more and more on the basis of past consensus decisions, the class creates and re-creates itself and its classroom culture.

To Doll, transformative possibilities emerge when reflection is "critical, public, and communal" (pp. 141-142). He defines these three attributes of reflection as ideal characteristics for the classroom and envisions a classroom as a communal place. His description matches closely what might occur in a classroom when a culture of consensus has become established.

> ...experiences could be openly analyzed and transformed; not a competitive environment where right is pitted against wrong, but one where, through mutual cooperation, students and teachers explore alternatives, consequences, assumptions. This communal and public exploration is done in a critical and rigorous yet sympathetic manner. Ideas are put forward for the purpose of

exploration, to be part of the recursive process.... Each party listens actively-sympathetically and critically- to what the other is saying. The intent is not to prove (even to oneself) the correctness of a position but to find ways to connect varying viewpoints, to expand one's horizon through active engagement with another. This engagement is a process activity, which transforms both parties. (pp. 142-150)

"The curricular challenge," Doll points out, "is to put this process into practical operation" (p. 142), which, he suggests, is no small challenge.

Connecting and transforming modernism with 'post' thinking will not be easy. Modernism is so well ensconced in our language and thought, that its most basic assumptions seem self-evident. It is only 'natural' to talk of imposing order, connecting effects with causes, transmitting ideas, and finding truth through scientific methodology.... The feature that I find most distinguishes the post-modern from the modern paradigm, and the one that also holds the most implications for curriculum, is self-organization.... Curriculum designed with self-organization as a basic assumption is qualitatively different from curriculum designed with the assumption the student is only a receiver. (pp. 157-159)

Teachers and students need to be free, encouraged, demanded to develop their own curriculum in conjoint interaction with one another. It is this curriculum development process via recursive reflection-taking the consequences of past actions as the problematic for future ones-that establishes the attitudes, values, and sense of community our society so desperately needs (p. 163). The focus would now be on a community dedicated to helping each individual, through critique and dialogue, to develop intellectual and social powers. (p. 174)

Consensus decision-making addresses this challenge squarely. Students "through critique and dialogue...develop intellectual and social powers." They continually work with "recursive reflection" as they examine the effects of their past decisions, and either continue or amend them to meet the changing situation. This process can allow a "self-organizing" curriculum to emerge and help "establish the attitudes, values, and sense of community our society so desperately needs."

Creating Cooperative and Multicultural Learning Communities

To construct cooperatively is to lay the foundations of a peaceful community
  (Sylvia Ashton-Warner, 1963).

It is not the individual as an isolated entity that is important but the person within the communal, experiential, and environmental frame
  (William Doll, 1993, p. 92).

Many educators today recognize a need for a different kind of classroom model, moving away from the authoritarian structure with the teacher transmitting what is to be learned to the students. Both K-12 and adult educators call for the creation of cooperative or collaborative learning communities whose members practice self-direction and self-responsibility while sharing the challenges of learning together and contributing their unique voices to the functioning of the community. This amounts to a wholly different approach to classroom management,, an approach that empowers every person in the classroom to participate in its management.

> ... AN APPROACH THAT EMPOWERS EVERY PERSON IN THE CLASSROOM TO PARTICIPATE IN ITS MANAGEMENT.

Learning communities are understood to go beyond intellectual or cognitive education; they support the emotional, social, and moral development of each member as well. Communication plays a key role. Consensus decision-making works especially well in learning communities because it also supports the multi-dimensional development of all participants and facilitates the growth of communication skills.

Caring and "Voice"

Nel Noddings (1992) believes that a school's first goal should be to promote the growth of students as healthy, competent, moral people. According to Noddings, teachers "have a responsibility to help their students develop the capacity to care" (p. 18) and yet she also notes that the structures of current schooling work against care (p. 20). She believes, "We need a scheme that speaks to the existential heart of life–one that draws attention to our passions, attitudes, connections, concerns, and experienced responsibilities" (p. 47). She believes we must help students to think of the school as theirs, and legitimize time spent in building relationships of care and trust (p. 174).

Ruth Charney (1991) emphasizes the importance of listening in "teaching children to care" (the title of her book).

> There is a vital relationship between the ways that teachers listen and talk, and the ways their children listen and talk. In both cases, we want to cultivate active listening, the action of hearing what others have to say, and showing that we hear and are trying to understand the intended meanings. Listening then becomes a willful act of respect and interest, rather than a passive stance of obedience.... Attentive love is an affection that allows us to look at children as more than beings to shape according to our own ideals and images. (pp. 125-126)

Lawrence A. Daloz (1986) concurs. "When the aim of education is understood to be the development of the whole person-rather than knowledge acquisition, for instance–the central element of good teaching becomes the provision of care rather than use of teaching skills or transmission of knowledge" (p. xvii). "Teaching," says Daloz, "is most of all a special kind of relationship, a caring stance in the moving context of our students' lives" (p. 14). He suggests that a teacher can provide a "potent tonic" by letting a student know that she or he matters enough to be cared about by someone important in the world (i.e. the teacher).

"To take the time and to let them know that they matter in this universe is a gift we can offer" (p. 240). Consensus decision-making operates on the premise that each person matters, that each person's needs and perspectives contribute to the wisdom of the whole.

Daloz cites *Women's Ways of Knowing* (Belenky, Clinchy, Goldberger, and Tarule, 1986) in emphasizing the importance of the development of "voice." In a second book, written ten years after the publication of *Women's Ways of Knowing* (WWK), Nancy Goldberger (1996)—one of its authors–reflects on what has happened since the earlier book and identifies the importance of both individual voice and learning in community. "...the most widely adopted design features from WWK are the concepts of voice and connection (connected knowing and connected teaching). Voice is related to the students' capacity to formulate and air their thoughts, believing they have something worthwhile to say, and feeling heard" (p. 41).

> CONSENSUS DECISION-MAKING OPERATES ON THE PREMISE THAT EACH PERSON MATTERS, THAT EACH PERSON'S NEEDS AND PERSPECTIVES CONTRIBUTE TO THE WISDOM OF THE WHOLE.

Conversation and dialogue are advanced as pedagogical practices that encourage engagement and quest and open new avenues to seeking truth through mutuality, reciprocity, and care rather than detachment and distance.... WWK has [provided] ...a means to integrate the inner voice and the voice of reason, and encourage a new kind of dialogue in the classroom.... Education is relational–a relationship that involves knowledge, attentiveness, and care; care directed not only at disciplinary material but to who students are and what they can become. (p. 45)

bell hooks (1994) developed the concept of "engaged pedagogy," a product of her thinking about education practices rooted in a respect for multiculturalism. In her writing, she also acknowledges the importance of caring and voice. "To teach in a manner that respects and cares for the souls of our students is essential if we are to provide the necessary conditions where learning can most deeply and intimately begin" (p. 13). "Engaged pedagogy necessarily values student expression" (p. 20).

hooks believes that one way to build community in the classroom is to recognize the value of each individual voice. She provides some added insights on the process of supporting students in coming to voice and also in listening to each other:

> Focusing on experience allows students to claim a knowledge base from which they can speak...Coming to voice is not just the act of telling one's experience. It is using that telling strategically–to come to voice so that you can also speak freely about other subjects. (p. 148)

> ....The more students recognize their own uniqueness and particularity, the more they listen. So, one of my teaching strategies is to redirect their attention away from my voice to one another's voices. (p. 151)

Building Learning Communities

Jill Tarule (1996) explores the paradigm shift that is called forth with the shift to a collaborative learning approach in the classroom:

> Within collaborative discourse, my particular concerns were integrating notions about relationships and the creation of classroom communities that transformed not only the conventional disciplinary boundaries, but also the ways students and faculty experience themselves as knowers.... Collaborative learning involves a distinct epistemology and pedagogy. It produces distinct outcomes and creates a distinctly different classroom culture than that of other more traditional approaches (Whipple, 1987). Collaborative learning "assumes that knowledge is a *consensus* among the members of a community of knowledgeable peers-something people construct by talking together and reaching agreement." (Bruffee, 1993, p.3)

> ...When collaborative procedures are introduced, they are not simply new "tricks" for teaching; they disrupt the basic assumptions about how learning progresses and who gets to be a knower.... In WWK [*Womens Ways of Knowing*], we describe how the "teacher as midwife" helps students give birth to and nurture their own voice and ideas, and about how connected teaching emphasizes believing students' ideas over doubting them, creating conditions for development that do not rely on competition or conflict to promote individuals' thought.... Groups led by a guide are different from groups led by an authority. The authoritative voice is no longer held by only one person; it is lodged in the discourse. (pp. 291-293, italics added)

> GROUPS LED BY A GUIDE ARE DIFFERENT FROM GROUPS LED BY AN AUTHORITY.

Tarule's description applies well to the consensus classroom, whether in an elementary school, a high school, a college or university.

hooks enters her college classroom with the assumption that "we must build 'community' in order to create a climate of openness and intellectual rigor (p. 39).... That has to be the starting point–that we are able to act responsibly together to create a learning environment" (p. 152).

> When I enter the classroom at the beginning of the semester the weight is on me to establish that our purpose is to be...a community of learners together. It positions me as a learner. But I'm also not suggesting that I don't have more power. And I'm not trying to say we're all equal here. I'm trying to say that we are all equal here to the extent that we are equally committed to creating a learning context. (p. 153)

hooks observes how learning in community generates excitement. "It is rare that any professor, no matter how eloquent a lecturer, can generate through his or her actions enough excitement to create an exciting classroom. Excitement is generated through collective effort" (p. 8). She also cautions: "The exciting aspect of creating a classroom community where there is respect for individual voices is that there is infinitely more feedback because students do feel free to talk—and talk back. And, yes, often this feedback is critical" (p. 42).

Like a consensus classroom, hook's "engaged classroom" is always changing. "When the classroom is truly engaged, it's dynamic" (p. 158). Although hooks writes here about college classrooms, her insights apply to other levels of education as well.

Cooperative Learning

Cooperative learning (Gibbs, 1994; Kagan, 1994; Kohn, 1992), which has been growing in popularity at the K-12 level of education, offers perspectives similar to those found in the above discourse on learning communities.

Alfie Kohn (1992) dispels myths that justify competition and calls for changing the structures that perpetuate it (p. 194). He points out that teachers of cooperative classrooms "recognize that 'socializing' is not something relegated to recess and lunch, something that detracts from learning; rather ... that learning emerges not only from what transpires between student and teacher, or between student and text, but also from what happens between student and student." The main problem in most schools, according to Kohn, is that students "do not find themselves part of a community of learners...[nor] in a place where each person's worth is affirmed" (p. 212). "A classroom that emphasizes and promotes the value of community—that has, in fact, been transformed into a caring community—allows positive interdependence to take hold" (p. 224).

Like many of the educators we cite, Kohn takes a constructivist position on teaching and learning:

> Here children are seen not as passive receptacles for facts but as beings who actively struggle to make sense of themselves and the world around them. This they do, in large part, by talking to others. Group discussion is not a 'bull session' during which students react to what they have already learned; this is where much of the learning occurs.
>
> The teacher's role is... to facilitate the process of playing with ideas and constructing meaning, and to aid in the development of intellectual and social skills. The goal is to get the student to develop an intrinsic, enduring commitment to this process (and to working successfully with others), to take responsibility for her [/his] learning and behavior. (p. 219)

Consensus decision-making helps students play with ideas, construct meaning, and develop intellectual and social skills while dealing with daily "real-life" issues in the classroom.

In his concern for diversity and meeting the needs of all students, Spencer Kagan (1994) cites four studies that examined and compared the gains of majority and minority students in traditional and cooperative classrooms. All found that minority students gained far more in cooperative than traditional classrooms.

One plausible explanation is the structural bias hypothesis. In brief, the hypothesis states that traditional classroom structures, because they rely heavily on competitive task and reward structures, provide a bias in favor of the achievement and values of majority students who are generally more competitive in their social orientation than are minority students. This hypothesis has received some support. Minority students, especially Hispanic students, are more cooperative in their social orientation than are majority students, and cooperative students achieve better and feel better about themselves and school in less competitive classrooms. (p. 2:7)

Kagan (1994), Kohn (1992), and Gibbs (1994) all refer to hundreds of lab and field research studies that demonstrate that cooperative learning has a number of positive outcomes. Among benefits reported, they identify: improved race-relations among students in integrated classrooms, increased individual and group productivity and academic achievement, constructive thinking skills, improved social and affective development among all students, a positive classroom climate, higher self esteem among students, internal locus of control, a sense of responsibility to other group members, more time on task, improved attendance, acceptance of mainstreamed students, and positive attitude toward school and learning.

> IN A CONSENSUS CLASSROOM, THE EMPHASIS IS ON WHOLE-CLASS COOPERATIVE WORK.

Kagan (1994) describes another positive outcome of cooperative classrooms:
> Students are allowed to do what they most want to do—communicate with their peers, and teachers are not forced to fight the natural tendencies of their pupils. The teacher in the cooperative classroom is on the same side as the student, serving not to dam up their natural expressiveness, but rather to channel it in positive directions. (p. 3:6)

In the cooperative learning literature, the emphasis is on small group cooperative work. In a consensus classroom, the emphasis is on whole-class cooperative work. In cooperative learning, "students spend most of their time in teams" (Kagan, p. 9:1), while in a consensus classroom as we conceive it, students spend some time working in teams but more of their group time working in the class as a whole.

In support of this whole-class emphasis, Kohn (1992) suggests that we move "beyond cooperative learning (at least in the way the concept is usually understood) and into the realm of what we might call the cooperative classroom" (p. 224). Kohn speaks to the "paradigm shift" that is required for a teacher who takes on cooperative learning (or, we might add, a consensus classroom):
> I am arguing that cooperation must come to be seen as a fundamental orientation toward other people rather than a set of techniques that are hauled out for specific lessons. This means working to change the feel of the classroom itself.... The whole atmosphere of the classroom from the time the kids get to school until the time they go home is based on the idea that you expect them

to get along, help each other, be cooperative... It means teachers must broaden their vision, rethinking the entire learning experience and working with students to fashion that experience into something that is cooperative inside and out. (pp. 224-225)

Kohn warns that teachers must give up predictability, noting that lack of predictability is not a necessary evil, but a requirement for learning. He quotes Eric Schaps (1990): "Deeper learning would look somewhat 'messier' than what I am seeing in most of our classrooms" (Kohn, p. 231).

Consensus vs. Majority Vote in Class Meetings

Ruth Charney (1991) believes that helping children learn to take better care of themselves, each other and their classrooms is probably the most enduring thing that we can teach. She also notes that teaching self-control and social participation takes time. "Without time in our day to talk to children and to allow them to talk to each other," she writes, "there will be no discipline, only disciplining" (p. 11). Many classrooms operating as cooperative learning communities utilize regular class meetings to ensure student participation and address "discipline" issues. Class meetings are also essential to consensus decision-making.

Kagan (1994) writes in support of class meetings:

> Regularly scheduled class meetings are one of the most powerful tools we have for teaching mutual respect, responsibility, caring, social awareness, cooperative attitudes, and democratic principles. The class meeting can also be a major source of support for the teacher as students actively strive to improve the class, find solutions to problems, and suggest consequences for behaviors. (p. 9:1)

Kagan points out two advantages of consensus decision-making over majority vote in class meetings: 1) voting can polarize a class, and 2) consensus places a powerful value on minority rights.

Jane Nelsen (1996) believes that "when more children (and adults) develop more social interest (concern for others, their community, and their environment) and learn methods and problem-solving skills to act on their concern, we will have peace in the world" (p. xix). Between the writing of the first and second edition of her book, Nelsen learned that "logical consequences" seldom need to be imposed—given a little training and guidance through class meetings, and faith in the ability of children to use their creativity to find solutions. Nelsen writes of "going beyond logical consequences":

> Even though an understanding of logical consequences can be helpful to teachers and students, I like to emphasize that it is important to focus on solutions instead of consequences. When given the opportunity [in class meetings], students can come up with a wealth of solutions that don't have anything to do with consequences. (p. 140)

In the first edition of her book, Nelsen suggested that class meeting decisions be made by majority vote; in the later edition, she mentions the possibility of consensus. The Developmental Studies Center (1996) favors consensus over majority vote, while acknowledging that it can be more challenging to reach a decision this way.

> Sometimes it is sufficient just to have brought up and discussed an issue raising everyone's awareness about it. But when a class does need to make a decision or resolve a problem, it is important that both teacher and students share a desire to reach consensus. When thirty-odd students are struggling with an issue, it can be tempting–for everyone involved–to seek the will of the majority by simply having students vote. The problem with voting, however, is that it tends to be a divisive experience that creates 'winners' and 'losers'–a distinction that significantly diminishes the sense of a caring community. The process of how a class arrives at a decision is as important as what the final decision is, and the process of consensus building is more responsive than 'majority rules' to the many voices within a group. The consensus-building process therefore not only reaffirms students' sense that their individual participation is meaningful and worthwhile, but also is invaluable in helping build their lifelong abilities of perspective taking and negotiation. (p. 36)

The Emerging Paradigm in Post-Modern Education

Jeanne Gibbs' (1994) "emerging paradigm" provides a summary of the ideas similar to those we have explored in this chapter. She ascribes to the emerging paradigm characteristics such as: emphasis on learning, emphasis on the whole, integrated knowledge and skills, student as active constructor of meaning, teacher as co-learner and facilitator, learning as a social activity, collaboration, student-directed learning, emphasis on process, learning grounded in "real world" contexts, open-ended and non-routine multiple solutions, shared development of goals and criteria for performance (p. 19). We believe all of these characteristics can be engendered through the use of consensus decision-making in the classroom.

In June, 1990, The Global Alliance for the Transformation of Education (GATE) brought together a group of holistic educators who eloquently outlined the educational challenges humanity faces in these post-modern times (Flake, 1993). They call for education to involve the enrichment and deepening of relationships to self, community, planet, and cosmos, and for human development to have priority over economic development.

> We call for each learner–young and old–to be recognized as unique and valuable. This means welcoming personal differences and fostering in each student a sense of tolerance, respect, and appreciation for human diversity. Each individual is inherently creative, has unique physical, emotional, intellectual, and spiritual needs and abilities, and possesses an unlimited capacity to learn.
> ... We suggest that we can build a true learning community in which people learn from each other's differences, are taught to value their own personal

strengths, and are empowered to help one another. As a result, each learner's individual needs will be met.

... We call for meaningful opportunities for real choice at every stage of the learning process. Genuine education can only take place in an atmosphere of freedom. Freedom of inquiry, of expression, and of personal growth is required. In general, students should be allowed authentic choices in their learning. They should have a significant voice in determining curriculum and disciplinary procedures, according to their ability to assume such responsibility.

... We call for a truly democratic model of education to empower all citizens to participate in meaningful ways in the life of the community and the planet. The building of a truly democratic society means far more than allowing people to vote for their leaders—it means empowering individuals to take an active part in the affairs of their community. A truly democratic society is more than the "rule of the majority"—it is a community in which disparate voices are heard and genuine human concerns are addressed. It is a society open to constructive change when social or cultural change is required.

In order to maintain such a community, a society must be grounded in a spirit of empathy on the part of its citizens—a willingness to understand and experience compassion for the needs of others.

... These are all educational tasks. Yet the teaching/learning process cannot foster these values unless it embodies them. The learning environment must itself revolve around empathy, shared human needs, justice, and the encouragement of original, critical thinking. Indeed, this is the essence of true education; it is the Socratic ideal, which has rarely been realized in educational systems. (pp. 241-244)

We believe that consensus decision-making in the classroom provides a structure that could go far toward answering these calls.

Involvement in the consensus process requires that we learn to let go of our attachment to particular outcomes. We discover that "success" may look very different than what we expect, that problems may be solved in ways we could never anticipate. I needed to constantly remind myself that the process was more important than outcome, and that my primary purpose was to empower my students to express themselves.

CHAPTER 5

Getting Started

Getting Started

Teachers interested in implementing consensus decision-making in their classrooms sometimes want specific "how to" advice; in this chapter, we offer a few examples as suggestions that may help you get started. Readers wanting more specific guidance in consensus practice may refer to the annotated list of resources at the end of the chapter. Some of the specific methods provided in the literature,

> **Journal Exercise: Goals And Resources For Implementing Consensus**
> (adapted from Macy & Brown, 1998)
>
> Answer each question in writing, or by speaking into a tape recorder. Write (or speak) as freely as you can, setting aside concerns about punctuation and grammar, so new ideas can readily emerge.
>
> 1. If you were liberated from all fear, open to all the power available to you within and beyond yourself, and were assured of the full support of your school administration and the parents of your students, how would you envision using consensus in your classroom? Pull out the stops on this one; put aside any fears or "practicality" for the moment.
> 2. In pursuing this vision, what could you accomplish realistically in a year's time? What steps can you take towards your vision?
> 3. What resources, inner and outer, do you now have that will help you move in this direction? Inner resources include specific strengths of character, and relevant experiences, knowledge, and skills you've acquired. External resources include relationships, contacts, and networks you can draw on, as well as your particular professional situation.
> 4. Now what resources, inner and outer, will you need to acquire? To do what you want to do, what will you need to learn and to obtain? These can run from attending consensus training, to joining an organization that uses consensus, to assertiveness training, to grants, to contacts in professional networks.
> 5. How might you stop yourself? What obstacles might you throw in the way of fulfilling your goal of implementing consensus in your teaching situation? We all have familiar patterns of self-doubt and sabotage.
> 6. How will you overcome these obstacles? Draw upon your past experience in dealing with these self-imposed obstacles, and perhaps some new ways of moving around them will occur to you.
> 7. What can you do in the next 24 hours, no matter how small the step–if only a phone call–that will move toward this goal?
>
> Read back your responses out loud to yourself, using the second-person pronoun: "You want to, you have, one way you might stop yourself," etc. Listen to yourself as if hearing, at long last, your orders from the universe.

however, may not be what is actually best for each particular group; if you try any, apply them with awareness of the unique factors of your situation. In preparing to introduce the idea of consensus decision-making to your class, we encourage you to journal about your own interests, expectations, feelings, doubts, concerns, limitations, and hopes. We also suggest that you try the exercise on the previous page to help clarify your goals and the resources you have available.

Getting the Idea Accepted in the Culture of the School

Teachers generally have some latitude in how they manage their classrooms, as long as their management systems remain within boundaries and expectations defined by state standards, district requirements, and school rules. Nevertheless, the culture of your individual school—and communications with parents, other teachers, and administrators—will affect the relative ease or difficulty of implementing consensus decision-making in your classroom.

As is probably true about anything you do in your classroom, having support of at least some of your administrators, fellow teachers, and your students' parents contributes greatly to the success of implementation. Thus, good communication is important. Share your intentions through conferences with your principal, brief presentations at faculty meetings and parent nights, and informal conversations with everyone. Through these communications, you can articulate why you are doing what you are doing, especially in terms of how it benefits the students. Although it may be difficult, it is probably most important to specifically elicit the concerns of those who apparently do not agree with your ideas. This will give you an opportunity to at least acknowledge—if not alleviate—their concerns and fears.

> ... CLASS TIME USED FOR CONSENSUS IS FULL OF LEARNING THAT FULFILLS SPECIFIC CURRICULAR REQUIREMENTS.

In Chapter 2, we addressed many of the benefits we see in using the consensus decision-making process in the classroom and you may find this useful in your own articulation. Remember that class time used for consensus is full of learning that fulfills specific curricular requirements. Consensus does not really use additional time. When Linda taught in California public schools, she justified class meeting time as relevant to both language arts and social studies. For language arts, class meetings provided an engaging and relevant way to practice speaking and listening skills. For social studies, the discussions and decisions provided students a direct experience of social studies concepts, including community development, problem solving, conflict resolution, interdependence, and governance. When consensus decisions were made within subject areas such as P.E. or literature, she could justify the time taken as developing motivation and understanding of the rationale behind the learning activities.

We recommend that you study your state and district guidelines to determine how class meetings and consensus decision-making activities fit within the required academic and social standards.

With the rise of high-stakes standardized testing throughout schools in the United States, teachers find themselves under increasing pressure. This can make using consensus in the classroom more of a challenge. Districts are increasingly dictating the pedagogy, thus limiting the decisions open to consensus. We hope the pendulum will soon swing back toward greater teacher autonomy, freeing teachers to rely once again on their own expertise and good judgment in determining how they work with their students.

To give you some ideas to get started, Linda describes how she introduced and guided the consensus process in her sixth grade classroom.

Introducing Consensus

I began my introduction to consensus by presenting my sixth grade students with a group challenge (Yurt Circle) on the first day of school. I also asked my students to come to a consensus decision about what to do for homework that night. Then in the morning of the second day, I guided the students through their first class meeting. Within the first week or two of school, I usually offered another consensus-building activity, "Coming to a Common Vision." I came to expect that at some point early on in the process—sometimes during the homework decision on the first day of school—there would be the "Inevitable Long Meeting" and/or a "Blocker" would emerge. So I mentally prepared myself for either possibility and left more flexibility in my lesson plans during those first few days of school.

Yurt Circle

In this group-challenge activity, students stand in a circle holding hands. There has to be an even number of participants, which determines whether or not the teacher joins the circle. Participants count off around the circle 1-2-1-2.... The object is for students to alternately lean in or out (ones lean in and twos lean out, for example) leaning from the ankles and keeping the rest of the body straight. When the challenge has been successfully completed, the participants balance each other around the circle so that each is standing in a position he or she could not be standing in alone. Once everyone is balanced, the group must count out loud together to 15.

I usually gave instructions and answered questions while we were still inside the classroom. Once outside I attempted to refrain from offering suggestions or answering questions.

One year the students were unsuccessful working in the large group and decided to divide into smaller groups, boys and girls. The girls almost succeeded but the boys mostly goofed around. I warned that if they had lost interest we would go back inside. Lacking leadership, the boys continued to goof off, so we went back inside. On the way in, I overheard some students wishing they could try it again, so once everyone was seated, I suggested that they talk about it. Doug said, "Raise your hand if you want to do the Yurt Circle again," and everyone raised their hands. Then I said, "OK, before we go out again, I want to hear some strategies." Karl noted that the boys were fooling around and that it might work better if the girls worked with the boys somehow. As they discussed the possibilities, I clarified and summarized the suggestions I was hearing. When it sounded like they were in agreement on a strategy, I repeated the strategy and checked for consensus. Then we did go out and try again, this time with more success, but they were unable to maintain the Yurt Circle to a count of 15.

I did this activity again toward the end of the school year so that the progress in the students' ability to work together was apparent. By then, the group just described was able to accomplish the task in a snap.

Introducing Consensus through the Homework Decision

In Chapters 2 and 3, I mention how my classes used consensus to decide on homework. Here I will give more specifics on that process. Since this was always the very first consensus decision my sixth and seventh grade students made, I would introduce the process by saying something like the following. "In this classroom, we will be making decisions using the consensus process. What I mean by consensus is that everyone agrees before a decision is final. Sometimes that takes a long time and sometimes it takes a short time." Then I told them that the first decision we would make this way was what we would do for tonight's homework assignments.

I would suggest a brainstorming session (see p. 44) and we would fill the blackboard with a list of ideas of what we could do for homework. Then I would guide the students in how to contribute to a consensus decision by saying: "It is important that each of us tells what we want and listens to every other person who speaks to hear what they want. Then while listening, we think, 'How can we solve it so everyone agrees?' Surprisingly enough, the more that people participate, the faster the decision can be made."

As the students commented on the brainstormed list, I asked them to keep in mind district requirements for homework at this grade level: between one and one-and-a-half hours per night supporting or practicing what we were learning in class. I suggested we could choose more than one learning activity. I placed stars next to the items that students named as something they would be interested in doing. Sometimes a new or combined item would be added in the process. I repeatedly reminded students to listen to each other and to seek what might work for everyone.

When I began to get a sense of what the students wanted I tried to articulate a proposal that included all of what I had heard up until that point in the discussion.

I might say something like, "It sounds like there is a lot of interest in [this] and [this]," to give them something concrete with which to work. Sometimes the first suggested proposal would be modified to include further individual needs and preferences as these emerged in the discussion. Sometimes a whole new proposal would emerge.

We would keep talking until we were all in agreement or until we ran out of time, in which case I would have to give the homework assignment based on what I had heard.

The First Class Meeting

I always scheduled the first official class meeting at the beginning of the second day of school, because there was already so much to do on the first day. As described in Chapter 3, I wrote the word "Agenda" on the board and let the students know that we would talk about anything that was important to them. I went on to say that we could make and change agreements "by coming to decisions using consensus, like we did for homework yesterday." I suggested that we might discuss: ideas for new ways of doing things or new things to do, complaints about the way things were, problems that anyone was having, or other changes that anyone wanted to make. "The way to go about getting help on a problem or making a change is to put it on the agenda and then, during class meeting time, we will talk about it. Remember, though, we can't change school rules or district requirements; so in the case of homework, for example, we can't choose not to do it."

> THE WAY TO GO ABOUT GETTING HELP ON A PROBLEM OR MAKING A CHANGE IS TO PUT IT ON THE AGENDA AND THEN, DURING CLASS MEETING TIME, WE WILL TALK ABOUT IT.

I called on students who had something they wanted to discuss and often they would just start talking about whatever was on their minds. I would then model how to give each concern a title and write that on the board under the word "Agenda." Once we had a list of topics, we would come to a consensus about which topic was the most important to discuss first and then proceed with that discussion. Any leftover topics at the end of the meeting would remain on the agenda. As mentioned in Chapter 3, I set aside a corner of the blackboard for class meeting agenda and students could add to it at any time.

At the beginning of any subsequent class meetings, we looked at what was on the agenda and came to a consensus about what was the most important thing to discuss first. This decision in itself could turn into a long discussion, but the students quickly realized that all the topics were important to someone and it made more sense to be talking about any one of them than to be spending a lot of time deciding which one to address.

I found it helpful to come up with suggested classroom guidelines prior to the first class meeting, in order to give students a starting place for discussion.

When I introduced these, I assured the students that the guidelines were all subject to change. I invited them to put on the agenda any guideline they wanted to discuss, or ideas for new guidelines.

Common Vision

During the first few days of school, I would schedule activities that developed a sense of community, such as the Yurt Circle described above (which physically embodies the consensus process) and a group envisioning process I call "Coming to a Common Vision." I initiated this activity by asking the students to write goals for themselves and then share them with the class. Taking everyone's individual goals into consideration, we would develop a statement of a common vision to which everyone would agree. We posted this statement on the wall next to the clock for the remainder of the school year where we could all see it and remind ourselves what we wanted to do together, whenever we seemed to be forgetting.

> ... WE LOOKED TO SEE WHAT COMMON VISION WE COULD ARTICULATE ...

Figure 2

> **COMING TO A COMMON VISION**
>
> Let's create a common vision–shared goals and an agreed way to work toward those goals–so we can all be clear about what we are trying to accomplish. Without a common vision, people often end up working at cross-purposes.
>
> **Vision** guides our actions to be in line with our deepest caring, our highest dreams.
>
> **Consensus** takes the dreams and hopes of each one of us into consideration.
>
> **Common Vision** emerges when we put together our personal dreams and goals as well as those of the class as a whole, to guide our actions in community.
>
> **To strengthen and improve our common vision:**
> 1. Talk about differences and concerns at the beginning.
> 2. Review agreements regularly.
> 3. Communicate to new members.
> 4. Periodically evaluate progress in relation to our clearly stated vision.
> 5. Ideally, each of us will be able to state our common vision and explain how decisions and actions fit the vision.

To initiate the process of developing a common vision, I hung a chart on the wall from the first day of school (Figure 2). I went over the chart and then had the students write goals for themselves for the school year (both for in class and on the playground). When I collected all their goals, I found that many of them were similar. Then I compiled a list that I thought included all of their personal goals, although some might have been stated slightly differently. When I presented the compiled list to the class, I asked them to check to make sure all their goals were included. Then together we looked to see what common vision we could articulate that would include everyone's goals.

One example of a common vision created in this way read, "We will work together to have a safe classroom and school, and we will support each other to get good grades and no detentions."

Common Challenges

Here are three challenges that I regularly faced in the early stages of consensus decision-making in my classroom, and how I learned to work with them. I hope my experience will help you prepare for similar problems that may emerge as you implement consensus in your classroom.

The Inevitable Long Meeting

Too often, a new consensus group gives up on using consensus too soon, due to "The Inevitable Long Meeting." The long meeting has occurred at least once (and usually only once) in every new consensus group in which I have participated. Whether with adults or children, the long meeting is often over a trivial issue that could be settled quickly by the authority figure in a non-consensus group. For example, early one year we spent two hours discussing what we were going to do for one hour of homework. Though frustrating, this long meeting is necessary for the shift in orientation in the participants, as they learn to respect and use their own power, and take a new kind of responsibility for their participation.

Expecting the long meeting can help you get through it when it occurs. It can be regarded as an initiation or rite-of-passage—celebrate its occurrence! Trust in the process develops over time.

Stuck in the Muck

When only one or two participants disagree with the proposal that emerges, finding out why and making an exception that works for everyone, or making a slight change in the plan, can usually resolve it. However, there are times when it is not so simple. Often, especially at first, the group seems divided into two or more camps, supporting specific options. Here are some of the ways my students and I have found to get unstuck:

- Ask to hear from more participants.
- Go around the room to hear from everyone.
- Stop to write in journals to get thoughts and feelings out (possibly stimulating fresh creative thinking), then report back to the group.
- Stop to pair up to share thoughts and feelings, then report back.
- Let the meeting time run out. A decision may come easily the next day.
- Decide to drop it for now and go on to another topic.
- Form a committee of those who have the strongest disagreement and highest interest to discuss and make a recommendation back to the class.

Molly used the following technique in her consensus-based cohousing community to help move participants through fears that seemed to be getting in the way of a particular decision. She invited community members to write their fears on slips of paper, using first person (e.g. "I am afraid that we will never find a solution and just go on talking endlessly"). She collected the slips in a basket, mixed them up, and passed the basket around the circle. Each person picked a slip at random from the basket and read it aloud. Everyone's fears were spoken, without anyone having to claim ownership of any particular one. The air felt clearer afterward, and the discussion continued productively with a more relaxed tone.

The Blocker

When someone says he/she disagrees, it is important to find out why. Through understanding the reason, individuals in the group can come up with ideas or ways to modify the plan that can accommodate the needs of the individual who disagrees. Especially at first, however, there is often someone who shows up as the one who always disagrees. Often in my classroom, one or more students would notice the pattern before I did and point it out. Feedback from the group was sometimes enough for the Blocker to recognize and change the pattern.

> EVERYONE'S FEARS WERE SPOKEN, WITHOUT ANYONE HAVING TO CLAIM OWNERSHIP OF ANY PARTICULAR ONE.

If pointing out the pattern was not enough, I learned to inquire whether or not the student could identify a need that he/she was expressing in this way. I was amazed that sixth graders actually grasped what I meant when I posed this question. Often the need was for attention or control. In either case, the whole class focusing on the one individual sometimes was enough to meet the need.

Such feedback from the group and/or the teacher might have embarrassed some students. Putting students in embarrassing situations is something I generally tried to avoid. However, if a student put him/herself in such a situation by his/her actions, I would let the natural consequences emerge. I have found that honesty and looking directly at the situation will often solve whatever problems arise.

Shifting from Being the Authority to Sharing the Authority

In Chapter 4 we discussed the postmodern paradigm shift in educational thinking that many teachers are experiencing within themselves and within their profession. Teachers who are considering making a shift towards consensus decision-making with their students will probably find that they must make their own internal paradigm shift from holding (or being) the authority to sharing the authority in their classrooms. Following are some ideas that might be helpful in working through this transition.

Over the years in my classroom, students asked to share–in several ways–the authority that is usually given to the teacher: leading class meetings, teaching art or other non-academic lessons, leading a PE or recreational activity, and teaching an academic lesson. I also found ways that I wanted to share authority, such as choosing who would receive citizenship and Student-of-the-Month awards, as provided by the school. Although you may not feel comfortable with any of these at first—and may never feel comfortable with some of them—you may want to start with one or two ways of sharing authority as possibilities occur to you or your students. Sometimes you gain comfort by trying.

When a new idea came, I found that it helped my comfort level if I was able to identify all my concerns and have them addressed by my students. For example, when a student first suggested the idea of students teaching academic lessons, I was not comfortable with it. It helped when I articulated my concern that the students might be disrespectful toward a peer teacher. Because they were excited about the idea and determined to make it work, they ended up being just as (if not more) respectful toward the student who was teaching as they were toward me.

In classrooms (as in many groups), control issues often lurk beneath the surface undermining the dynamics of the relationships, both at the individual and group level. The consensus process tends to bring such underlying dynamics to the surface. As mentioned in Chapter 2, authority issues sometimes emerge as power struggles in which everyone loses, and it may take a while to recognize the authority issues at the heart of the conflict. By confronting the power struggle directly, and exploring with the students the underlying authority issues, the teacher can help the group free itself from this entanglement and find a resolution through which everyone wins.

On at least one occasion I recall, I was caught in a power struggle myself. I arbitrarily asserted my authority as a teacher, and later regretted it. A small group settled to meet around a desk that belonged to a student who was not present in the classroom. I objected, and the students politely questioned why. When I explained, they took my concern into consideration and came up with a way to address it. Yet I stayed embedded in my position that they move elsewhere until they complied. Upon reflection later, I recognized that I had not acted in accordance with my commitment to empower my students to develop their internal authority.

In contrast, I remember another time when I regretted not having asserted more authority. When my students were planning a party, I did not speak up about how important I thought it was for someone to be directing activities at any given time—someone to whom the others could look for directions. At one point during the party, enthusiasm was high and the noise level was rising. I began feeling that things had become so chaotic that the class needed direction, but there was no one in the position to give it. The students could not hear each other or me, they ended up yelling at each other, and the situation was "out of hand" as far as my comfort level was concerned.

I have learned that in order to find a balance between the unsatisfactory extremes of domination on the one hand and chaos on the other, I need to be clear in each situation about my boundaries and the values behind these boundaries. I really need to know what is okay and what is not okay with me, and why. In the desk situation above, I was not clear on what was really important to me and got stuck in a rigid position that seemed a bit like "Do what I say because I say so." I held on to what I later determined was too much control. In the party situation, I had not been clear about my boundaries during the planning stage, so during the party itself, I found myself in a situation that felt too chaotic.

In learning to clarify my boundaries, I noticed that my tendency was to enter a discussion with preconceived limits in mind, taking a rather defensive stance. I came to realize that if I were clear about the wants, needs, or other concerns that were behind my preconceived limit, I had more opportunity to be flexible. When I was able to express my concerns without necessarily having already worked out the solutions, I often found that my students had great ideas that would not have occurred to me. I also began to ask the students to explore the wants, needs, and other concerns behind their positions. Together we discovered ways to have all of our concerns addressed.

> ... I OFTEN FOUND THAT MY STUDENTS HAD GREAT IDEAS THAT WOULD NOT HAVE OCCURRED TO ME.

Sometimes as part of our planning discussion–as in the one about students teaching academic lessons–I expressed all my concerns and thus together my students and I were able to establish clear boundaries. At such times, because my concerns were obvious to me from the beginning, they were easy to identify and include in the discussion. Other concerns–as in the party incident–arise in hindsight and may be helpful the next time around. Such ups and downs can be expected as we learn from our mistakes.

Journal Exercise: Clarifying Needs

Entering a discussion with some understanding of your own wants and needs makes it more likely that they will be met. Clarifying the need underneath a limit that you are tempted to set may allow you to be more flexible in finding solutions that meet your needs and everyone else's. The following questions may be helpful to address when something new appears on the agenda.
• What are your personal limits or tolerances in this area?
• What might be the fears, need(s), or want(s) underlying the above limits or tolerances?

Encouraging Self-Expression

In an attempt to accommodate the comfort level of others, many of us restrict our own freedom of self-expression and spontaneity. However, I have found that the more comfortable I am with my own spontaneity, the more others seem to feel free to express themselves as well. One of the challenges in initiating consensus in the classroom, is to help students feel comfortable with self-expression, contributing both feelings and ideas to class discussions.

As we have said, expressing feelings is an essential part of the consensus process. Everyone's feelings affect their preferences and thus the final consensus. Unexpressed feelings can be particularly troublesome because they can block clarity and derail a decision. Encouraging the expression of feelings may be challenging at first because many of us have been conditioned to hide our feelings, especially in a public situation like school. Framing the expression of feelings as a contribution to the group can help reassure yourself and your students. Even so, some feelings are easier to express than others—and there may be some feelings that you are not willing to express at all.

I found it difficult to express hurt feelings in my classroom because I felt so vulnerable. During my most difficult year, I felt hurt quite often and I finally spoke about it during a class meeting, which led to a discussion about abuse. As a class, we came up with a way to talk about hurt feelings that I think may be helpful to other classes. Our agreement was actually a take-off on the disturbance rule (see p. 47): let the other person know if he/she said or did something that hurt your feelings; listen to someone if he/she says you did something that hurt his/her feelings; and stop saying or doing that sort of thing to that person after being told that it hurt his/her feelings.

At first, many students may be reluctant to speak up about their ideas as well as their feelings; some students remain reluctant all year. Here are some approaches I have found helpful for eliciting student input:
- Ask for suggestions before (or instead of) making suggestions.
- Ask why when someone disagrees with a decision.
- Encourage students to search their personal experience and/or check within when looking for answers or solving problems.
- Validate each contribution.
- Acknowledge the challenge when a decision is not coming easily, and affirm that the students are doing well when they remain focused on the discussion.
- Accept all students' contributions the way they are, even though some may be less vocal than others.

Remember that the teacher is not the only repository of information. There is no absolute authority for what is right and what will work.

Process and Outcomes

Involvement in the consensus process requires that we learn to let go of our attachment to particular outcomes. We discover that "success" may look very different than what we expect, that problems may be solved in ways we could never anticipate. I needed to constantly remind myself that the process was more important than outcome, and that my primary purpose was to empower my students to express themselves. Keeping these priorities clearly in mind—in concert with awareness of my own needs, wants, limits, and tolerances—enabled me to remain flexible and to contribute to consensus discussions without undue investment in having my own ideas accepted.

Getting started using consensus in the classroom is an exciting and potentially rewarding adventure. At the same time, the process can also bring up fears and resistance in ourselves and others. Resistance seems to come up when people are about to change. "Resistance is a signal...that idols are toppling, that a world view or identification is threatened. We need to understand this in our own process, as well as in [others]" (Brown, 1983). The consensus process challenges some long-held assumptions about authority and power. If you can accept resistance as part of the process—listening to and honoring others' (and your own) concerns—you may weather the storms with more equanimity. Take it slowly, with compassion for yourself, your students, their parents, and the rest of the school community.

It is also quite possible that your venture will be met with enthusiasm by students, parents, and faculty alike, because consensus seems to meet a deep human need to be heard, and to have one's needs and preferences included in decisions.

We hope our words have helped inspire you to launch your own grand experiment in democracy.

CONSENSUS RESOURCES

Butler, C.T. (1987). *On conflict and consensus.* Food Not Bombs Publishing. www.consensus.net.
> On this website, Butler codifies a formal structure for consensus decision-making with a particular emphasis on encouraging conflict as a desirable element. The structure of "Formal Consensus" has three levels: 1) broad open discussion; 2) identification of concerns; and 3) resolution of concerns. Six "Rules" are identified, particular roles are defined, and many techniques are briefly described.

Crosby, R.P. (1998). *The authentic leader: How authority and consensus intertwine.* Seattle, WA: Skaya Publishing.
> Crosby writes to an audience who is interested in leadership in organizations, telling stories about ways people have effectively blended consensus and authority.

Hunter, D., A. Bailey and B. Taylor (1997). *Co-operacy: A new way of being at work.* Fisher Books.
> The authors describe frameworks, methods, and processes that support whole-person, cooperative, peer partnerships. Co-operacy is defined as the technology of collective or consensus decision-making. This book includes a section on introducing co-operacy, another section on applying it, and a final section with 61 processes.

Saint, S. and J. R. Lawson (1994). *Rules for reaching consensus: A modern approach to decision making.* San Diego, CA: Pfeiffer & Company.
> This book, a concise 71 pages, is very much a "how to" with a step-by-step process. We agree with many of the recommendations but not with all of them.

Scott, J. and E. Flanigan (1996). *Achieving consensus: Tools and techniques.* Menlo Park, CA: Crisp Publications, Inc.
> A visually fun, workbook style "how to," this book defines consensus, explains individual roles in creating consensus, shows the steps needed, and provides problem-solving tools and techniques.

Tagliere, D.A. (1993). *How to meet, think, and work to consensus.* San Diego, CA: Pfeiffer & Company.
> This book is really more about getting a team working together than it is specifically about consensus decision-making.

Afterword

We want to acknowledge that, because education is compulsory, children have no voice in whether or not they attend school. If their parents have the necessary resources, they can choose private or home schooling, but children must be involved in some sort of formal educational process—by law. It may seem like a huge contradiction to impose consensus decision-making on an essentially captive audience, but teachers all use some sort of decision-making process to manage their classrooms, whether it be authoritarian, majority rule, individual contracts, or consensus. We believe there is an innate desire to learn in all of us, but authoritarian approaches often block it. Students may not even experience their own desire to learn when teachers and parents make decisions for them. The consensus decision-making process builds on this innate desire by offering students the opportunity to contribute to decisions that determine their learning environment. Given that students are stuck in the classroom six to seven hours a day, five days a week, for nine months, consensus is a powerful way to make the best of the situation: it supports students and teachers in creating together a learning environment that works for everyone.

As educators ourselves, we are increasingly alarmed about the trend in the United States to measure outcomes and results, quantitatively, and assume those as the only ways to evaluate education. We believe schools would do well to also examine the *means* for education, asking these kinds of questions:

- Are the means congruent with our deepest understandings of how people learn?
- Do they reflect the latest scientific findings in how the brain functions?
- Do they respect cultural and individual differences?
- Do they help children learn at their own paces, in their own styles?
- Are they democratic?
- What are we teaching by *how* we are teaching?

We believe that consensus decision-making provides a structure for continually examining the means for education, rooted in the aliveness of day to day classroom experiences.

We invite you to use these ideas in whatever way works for you and your classes, and let us know about your experiences—share what you have learned and/or ask for our advice. We see this (and all of our teaching) as a work in progress, and we would love to continue to learn from everyone's experiences. Keep in touch!

Linda Sartor, *lsartor@inreach.com,* 7899 St. Helena Road, Santa Rosa CA 95404.

Molly Young Brown, *molly@mollyyoungbrown.com,* P.O. Box 1301, Mt. Shasta, CA 96067.

Consensus Classroom, Inc. (CCI) is a tax-exempt non-profit organization with a mission to empower students to take responsibility for themselves, their classroom environment, and their lives; and to facilitate communication using the consensus process. This organization has produced an amateur video that shows the consensus process in action in two of Linda Sartor's classrooms (2nd grade and 6th grade). Colleagues and ex-students are also interviewed about their experience of the consensus classroom. The video provides a visual experience to expand upon the descriptions in this book. Cost: $10.

For more information about CCI or how to order the video tape, contact:

Consensus Classroom, Inc.
7899 St. Helena Rd.
Santa Rosa, CA 95404
707-538-5123

Appendix

Katherine Kennedy: Another Teacher's Story

Katherine Kennedy has used consensus decision making in her third grade class at the International School of Helsinki. Katherine took an Internet course from Linda on the using consensus in the classroom, read an earlier draft of this book, and watched the Consensus Classroom video. She has generously given her permission to share a report she prepared as well as excerpts from her journal, to give readers a glimpse into another consensus classroom in action.

Katherine's Report

I teach a third grade class at the International School of Helsinki. Our school is located on the coast of Finland. My class is made up of fourteen children from ten different countries. Only three students have English as their mother tongue. I introduced the consensus classroom to my students when we began the second semester of our school year.

I have found that the consensus classroom enables students and teachers to develop daily life skills that can be used both inside and outside of the classroom. Students are taught problem solving skills, communication skills and are empowered to speak up for their beliefs. At the same time, teachers are able to develop both time management skills and communication skills. Implementing the consensus classroom has increased participation in all areas of study and developed an enthusiastic learning environment.

When beginning the consensus classroom, the students discussed the definition of the word consensus. As a class we defined consensus to mean, "everyone is in agreement with the final decision." The consensus classroom allows equal decision making power between the teacher and the students. It was then stated that if we were not in agreement with a particular decision we would work together until the entire group reached a consensus. I was skeptical at first and envisioned hours of negotiating solutions to problems. Luckily, this was not the case!

Class Meetings

Our daily class meetings were used as a time to solve problems and share ideas. In our meetings the students were told that everyone would have an opportunity to share their opinions and no one would judge the opinions of others. Students learned that we may often have different opinions but that being different does not necessarily mean being wrong. The class meetings enabled students to hear and value different opinions

I took the opportunity to ask my students how they felt about having class meetings each day. Stephanie expressed that she enjoyed class meetings and said, "People get to talk about what is bothering them and no one can tell them they are wrong." Repeatedly students stated that they liked having a scheduled time to resolve problems that occurred within the classroom as well as problems that developed outside the classroom. Lisa said, "I like having class meetings because we can work out problems and everyone has a chance to say something about the subject."

I also asked the students, "Do you think it is a good idea to have everyone reach a consensus before we make a final decision?" Can (pronounced "John") explained his answer by saying, "Yes, I think it is a good idea. It helps us solve our problems and we stick by the decision." When students are part of the decision making process, they are more likely to participate in the activity. I found that I did not have to take extra time during lessons to generate enthusiasm and participation amongst the class. Lisa said, "When we reach a consensus no one has a bad feeling about an activity." Several students stated that when we reach a consensus everyone is much happier with the decision and no one feels "left out." Reaching a consensus as a group leads to participation from all the members in the class.

> OFTEN, WHEN THE CLASS IS WORKING TOWARD A CONSENSUS, NEW IDEAS EMERGE.

Class meetings allow the students a safe environment to openly express their disagreements. Tuija stated that she thought that it was a good idea to reach a consensus in the class meeting because, "No one is screaming 'I want to do that!'" We all sit together peacefully to work toward a solution we are all able to agree upon. The students are encouraged to listen to one another and to share their opinions with the group. Listening is a language skill that children rely upon during their early school years. When reaching a consensus, teachers are able to identify those students who were not listening. Class meetings promote active listening in the classroom. A final decision can not be made unless all members of a group are listening attentively.

Often, when the class is working toward a consensus, new ideas emerge. If someone is not in agreement with an idea, we all try to convince the individual why it is a good idea or we offer alternative activities. Tuija said, "When trying to reach a consensus, we see what everyone wants and we find new ideas." An example would be the class meeting during which Can did not want to play any of the three physical education games the class had agreed upon. As a member of the group I offered to participate in the game and allow Can to be our teacher. This was a wonderful opportunity for Can to lead a group activity and it allowed the teacher a chance to work along side of the students.

Our daily class meeting enabled the students to share suggestions for activities in all subject areas. During our social studies lessons on Asia, I was able to have two students lead activities. Natsuka patiently taught the class how to create Origami artwork and the students were shown how to write their names in Japanese. Ashish introduced the class to a game played by children in India and shared letters from the Hindu alphabet. During a language arts lesson, Stephanie taught a spelling game to the class. We have continued to use this game as a review for our weekly spelling assessments. Each one of these lessons allowed the class to learn something new and at the same time gave these three students an opportunity to practice speaking in front of a large audience.

Speaking Up Can Lead to Change

The consensus classroom is set up in a way that makes students feel free to speak up for their beliefs. They are empowered to share their knowledge and feelings about all issues. Students in the consensus classroom do not sit silently when they are opposed to an idea. Frequently, their opposition to an idea leads to change.

One afternoon my students returned from recess extremely upset because they were no longer allowed to play in a specific area of the playground. Instead of complaining that life was not fair and remaining angry, several students placed the issue on our agenda. Together we listed specific reasons why the class wanted to use the playground area and then listed suggestions on how we could implement change. Three students brought our proposal to the principal and after talking with the headmaster and the park department, the students were allowed to use the playground area again. Our class meeting led to another solution for a problem outside of our classroom.

> THE CONSENSUS CLASSROOM IS SET UP IN A WAY THAT MAKES STUDENTS FEEL FREE TO SPEAK UP FOR THEIR BELIEFS.

Time Management

The students are not the only individuals who benefit from the consensus classroom. Teachers are offered the opportunity to learn from their students and develop a mutual respect for one another. One skill that I surprisingly developed during implementing the consensus classroom was time management.

An agenda was posted permanently on the front board in my classroom. This allowed the students, teacher, and teacher aide a place to write topics they wished to discuss with the group. We would begin each class meeting by agreeing on the order in which we would address the topics. Victor said he thought it was a good idea to have an agenda because, "We can organize our time." The agenda enabled us to prioritize issues and to set aside time for discussions.

The students all enjoyed the opportunity to have a place to post their concerns where everyone could see them. Stephanie stated, "I think it is a good idea to post an agenda because people can see what we are talking about before our meeting." I also enjoyed preparing for topics that I thought might lead to lengthy discussions. One afternoon I noticed that "table manners" had been placed on the agenda. I was able to prepare some handouts and activities on the topic before our next meeting, only because it was posted on the agenda. Natsuka said, "I like having an agenda because some other students might have some questions about the topic."

Before I began holding class meetings, many of the agenda topics were dealt with at an individual level. By placing problems on the agenda I no longer had to make time to resolve conflicts individually. In the consensus classroom the students assist the teacher in solving problems. Many conflicts are resolved in class meetings and I no longer find myself alone with a group of children trying to resolve a conflict. I have found that I now have more teaching time and spend less time trying to work out conflicts amongst students.

Our posted agenda also served as a place to remind each other of upcoming events. It allowed us the opportunity to record an item we thought was important and we were afraid we might forget to share. An example would be when Tuija placed "Earth Day" on the agenda. I was caught up in planning events for "Young Author's Week" and almost forgot one the most important events in school. Thanks to a student and our agenda we were able to plan several fun and informative activities for Earth Day.

> IN THE CONSENSUS CLASSROOM THE STUDENTS ASSIST THE TEACHER IN SOLVING PROBLEMS.

Homework was a weekly topic on the agenda. Each Monday we would discuss our lessons for the week and try and arrange our homework accordingly. Reviewing the homework for the entire week helped the students work on time management skills. We would review suggestions from both the teacher and the students for various homework topics. Next, we would discuss what day an assessment might take place. After finalizing the homework schedule, the students were allowed the opportunity to turn assignments in early. Assigning the homework for an entire week helped me stay on schedule with the corresponding lesson plans.

Listening to Students

Daily class meetings allowed me the opportunity to listen to my students. Listening is a skill that I needed to develop and through class meetings I have improved in this area. I found that, before we began class meetings, I did not always take the time out of my schedule to sit down and listen to every problem my students brought to me. Tuija stated, "The teacher is never too busy to discuss something on the agenda; it will get discussed."

The class knows that I will listen to each concern written on the agenda and it will be discussed until a solution has been found. If a solution is not found during one meeting we will carry on with the discussion at our next class meeting. The students may use their free time to brainstorm solutions and address the group at our next meeting. Everyone understands that if they have a problem and need to spend time discussing a solution they can place the item on our agenda. Maja said, "If there was no agenda, then the time would be limited." Yes, our class meetings do have a time limit; however, there is not a time limit for how long a topic can stay on our agenda.

Starting a consensus classroom has helped me grow professionally and personally. I have learned how to communicate better with my students and colleagues.

I have also used the class meetings and agenda items to help me organize activities in the classroom. The students will be leaving third grade as better communicators and problem solvers. They will also take with them the knowledge that speaking up for what you believe in can lead to a positive change. My students now realize that they deserve the right to be heard. I look forward to continuing my career as a teacher in a consensus classroom.

Katherine's Journal (Spring 1999)

Some of the material in Katherine's journal is redundant, as she reported on it above. We include it here to provide the reader with a sense of her process through the semester.

March 2

Yesterday we brainstormed different possible homework assignments. I soon realized that certain students felt strongly about which days certain assignments were due. After discussing this, I noticed that some students were a little stressed on the days they had an after school activity (piano or dance lessons). We came to a consensus that all homework for the week would be discussed and posted on the board each Monday. Students could choose to complete assignments earlier in the week if they were busy later in the week. During our class meeting, students talked about their desire to teach a lesson to the class. Natsuka, a Japanese student, has decided to teach a lesson related to our topic on Asia. We visited the library and looked at several options. She decided that she will teach the class how to make an "Origami Flapping Bird."

March 3

Today we spent a great deal of time trying to reach a consensus on which dessert we will be baking next week. We finally had to narrow down our options to help us reach a consensus. The class decided what activity they would like to have Natsuka teach the class. In our class meeting we came up with several new activities the students could take part in during our "Friday Free-time." The students offered suggestions that I would have not thought of by myself.

March 8

When reviewing the book [an early draft of *Consensus in the Classroom*], I noticed that brainstorming is an area that I need to work on. I found that I (not just the students) have a tendency to evaluate an item when it is first suggested. When a good idea is brought forth, I naturally praise the idea. I think that now that I am aware of this, I will be able to write a brainstorming list without evaluating.

I know I mentioned this before, but I am really pleased with the fact that I am becoming a better listener. Well, actually I am just allowing my students the opportunity to share their opinions and they weren't really given many opportunities to do this before we had scheduled class meetings. On Friday I wrote about how the students' suggestions have lead to me feeling more organized. They have suggested procedures that I have thought of implementing but never got around to following through with. Thanks to the students we have sign up sheets for different activities to make sure everyone has a turn to participate.

March 9

We have had a very exciting day with the visiting astronaut. The students had to come to a consensus on what we could do related to the astronaut's visit. They decided to brainstorm interview questions, hold an interview, and then write an article about what was discussed. The class wasn't as excited today about coming to a consensus on homework. I had them stop in the middle of our meeting to do exercises. I think they were half-asleep. No one could think of any agenda items during our class meeting, so we focused on the two topics I had mentioned. We only discussed one and I will discuss "Music Class" tomorrow. There is a long-term substitute in Music and their behavior could be much better.

March 10

On the agenda today was unresolved conflicts. The teacher assistants go outside with the students for recess. I am not always made aware of conflicts that arise outside and apparently something happened yesterday at recess that this child was still concerned about. She wanted to know what to do when a conflict was not resolved using the "peace wheel." The class discussed how both people need to be willing to work out a problem and that perhaps we need to have a mediator sit with them when they are working to resolve a conflict. I suggested we use the "conflict resolution process" [see p. 49] if the peace wheel does not work. The girls did not want to work out the problem in front of the class and we decided to let them work in private using the process. We went over the steps and a student typed them up for me to laminate. This process is rather similar to my peace wheel, I think; the only difference is that you have to restate the other person's views when using the peace wheel.

I think the conflict resolution process worked well in a group setting and took less time, but I will continue to use the peace wheel as well. It is a circle that is turned behind a window and you may rotate the circle to see different steps in the window. The steps:

1. Each person takes a turn saying the rules. (The negotiation rules are on a poster:
No interrupting. No name-calling or put-downs. Work to resolve the conflict).
2. Decide who goes first
3. Person #1 tells what happened
4. Person #2 restates and asks how #1 feels
5. Person #2 tells what happened
6. Person #1 restates and asks how #2 feels
7. Person #1 gives a solution
8. Person #2 agrees or gives another solution. Each person should win!
9. Each person states the solution

10. Each person states what can be done so that the problem DOES NOT happen again! (This activity may be geared more for upper elementary students).

March 11

We finished up our center activities today. I was extremely pleased with Natsuka taking responsibility for teaching a group this week. She was very patient teaching Origami to her classmates. We are discussing "stress" in science and it was interesting for her to talk about how calm and relaxed you must be to participate in this activity. She said that her mother often makes her go ride her bike if she is not calm and relaxed enough to begin Origami.

I used the conflict resolution process to help resolve a conflict yesterday and it worked rather well. I was sitting with five children in a guided reading group when I noticed a boy (Can, pronounced "John") was crying. I told him we could not continue to read if he was this sad. We went over the four steps to resolving conflicts with him and then called Stuart over to join us. Stuart and Can are best friends and rarely have disagreements. Well, they both went through the steps, with tears dripping down their faces. When they had finished the steps, Tuija ran and got Kleenex; I had tears in my eyes now, too, and Paul said, "I think you need to shake hands or hug now." I was really glad I stopped my reading group to deal with this misunderstanding.

March 15

It is nice that I keep finding answers to many questions as I read over *The Consensus Classroom* [an earlier draft of this book]. I was just looking at my book and saw "a class-planned activity." It made me think about our class meeting tomorrow. My class has earned 25 marbles for good behavior and will have a "Marble Day" next week. This is a student planned day and tomorrow they can choose the activities for our marble day. In the past I have voted against several activities (example: swimming) but after using consensus in the classroom, I feel that I need to be more open minded to activities. If it is something reasonable and they really want to do it, I should go along with the activity. I really enjoy having class meetings! Today Ashish said that he would like to teach the class a game from India when we have center activities. The students enjoyed having Natuska teach last week and who is better qualified to talk about Asia than my students from these countries.

March 16

Today was the longest class meeting we have had so far. The students had to decide on what to do for their "Marble Day." I did a good job at not evaluating any suggestions. I even wrote "buying a dog" on the board. Of course the students quickly decided this was not a realistic option. We had a long discussion on swimming vs. a movie and pizza. After hearing many views, it was decided that we will order pizza and watch a movie. The students are now hoping to work toward having a "Marble Day" in June and go swimming when it is warmer outside. One down side to swimming was that it would take a long time to blow dry everyone's hair. Our class meeting then went into a huge discussion on what movie to watch. The students are 8 and 9 years old and don't see any problem with watching a PG-13 movie. After brainstorming many options we decided to think about it some more and continue the discussion tomorrow at our class meeting.

March 17

When we had our class meeting yesterday, I noticed the teacher assistant making faces when someone suggested going swimming. It occurred to me that we had not been encouraging her to take part in our meetings. She is not with us everyday, but we now have her participating in discussions when she is present.

I am voicing my concerns at meetings, but I worry that sometimes I might have too much influence. Example: I wasn't really keen on swimming and I did an excellent job of bringing up all the negative aspects of a swimming trip.

At our class meeting today, we continued to discuss what movie to watch on our "Marble Day." The students agreed that they were not 13 and they understood why I did not feel a PG-13 movie would be appropriate. Next, we had a big discussion on scary movies. We talked about how people have different views on what is scary and that we need to respect these views. I told the students that we would not make a final decision on a movie until Monday (our "Marble Day" will be Wednesday). I asked the students to talk with their parents about what they think would be a good "Third Grade Movie".

Today we have another staff meeting. I really want the meetings to end earlier and this usually only happens when we don't all talk or voice our opinions. Many times I keep my opinions to myself and then go home and complain to my boyfriend. Reading *The Consensus Classroom* helped me realize that it is important to voice one's opinion or concerns. I just hope today that I agree with everything so we can go home early!

March 18

I know I keep saying this, but I really do love these class meetings! Generally I do not teach any structured PE lessons. The kids have recess daily with the teacher assistants and PE lessons with a teacher 3 days a week. This week the PE teacher will be gone on Friday and said I could use the gym with my class. I remembered the part in the consensus video when the class decides on a PE activity. I thought we could brainstorm games for our PE lesson. I caught myself saying something when "American Football" was mentioned; I started to blurt out an objection. We narrowed it down to either playing three short games or one game of basketball. Can (John) was the only person who wanted to play basketball and was adamant about not participating in the other games. I thought back to the video and asked if he would like to be our referee. I told him I would give him a whistle and that I would also like him to give instructions for each game to the class. We decided I would participate in the games and I would also need to be told the instructions. I told him that I would like the class to do exercises first and if he wants to, he may lead the class in those as well. He is very excited about our PE lesson tomorrow!

Yesterday I wrote about how my teacher assistant participated in our class meeting. I have a teacher assistant who is here half days and a personal aide who is in the room everyday. She works with an emotionally disturbed/learning disabled child who is an active member in the class. She leaves the class for a 15-minute break in the morning and an hour break when Paul visits the LD [Learning Disability] teacher. She also goes outside everyday and observes many things on the playground and special classes that I do not see. The assistants are not always present for the class meetings and generally have not participated until yesterday (and today). Today the personal assistant asked if we could add "lining up" as a topic for our agenda. She said this has been a hot topic and that it causes many conflicts. We discussed the issue and the class came up with two rules. They are: 1) No saving places; 2) If you leave the line for something you forgot, you may not go back to your spot.

Stephanie did not agree with rule #2 because she said it didn't bother her. We had about 6 different children speak to her directly about why it was a good rule. After they spoke we raised hands to see if we could come to a consensus. Stephanie was now in agreement. I asked what changed her mind. She said that it still didn't bother her but she now realized it really upset a lot of students when people left their spots in line and tried to return. The personal assistant just thanked me for letting her bring this up. I told her that I should thank her.

March 19

What a busy day! I am still a little winded from our PE lesson. We had a great time with Can being the referee. I brought in PE clothes and changed with the girls in the locker room. I was a student and Can was the PE teacher. He did a nice job leading us in exercises and two games. I had to settle the class down a couple of times but they did a nice job listening to Can. We were all exhausted from all the running. The kids loved having me participate in the games. I never would have thought of doing this activity if it wasn't for this course.

March 22

Well, I hope my week gets better. Paul (an American student with emotional and learning problems) tried to beat up Can today on the playground. Can said he is mad at himself because he hit Paul back and he has never hit anyone in his life. Oh...was it last week I said there are virtually no discipline problems in our school? The principal is in India and I just found out that there is no policy on fighting in our school because it rarely happens. Paul has difficulty controlling his anger and his personal assistant said he became extremely frustrated because he wasn't part of a group of boys playing (he actually told me he was so angry because their voices were too loud and disturbing him in line). Can and Paul sat through a peace wheel discussion. I was so angry with Paul and I guess this was obvious because Can kept saying that I should be mad at him too. I told them I was disappointed in them both. They are writing letters to each other tonight and I guess we can talk more about conflicts in a class meeting tomorrow. I think I need time to cool off more than the boys.

March 23

[Katherine sent Linda her journal entries via e-mail as part of her course work. The following is Linda's e-mail response to the previous journal entry.]

It may be a great learning experience for everyone in your class to take the situation of Paul and Can and discuss it—if it is okay with Paul and Can. Students can put themselves in the positions of the two boys and talk about how they would feel. Then they might discuss/brainstorm what sort of things they could do if they were in such a situation. It would be important to set up such a discussion in a way that everyone realizes that there are many ways to deal with any situation but that some ways open up communication better than others. There isn't one right way.

I wouldn't want the boys to be embarrassed further by feeling that what they had "done wrong" was made so public. They did what they did and have felt the pain of it as a consequence. This isn't meant to be further punishment but a good learning opportunity. As part of the conversation, both boys could tell how they felt and how they now feel and they might feel better if they realize that others might have similar feelings. The discussion might open up some possibilities for everyone to which they wouldn't otherwise have had access.

By acknowledging the truth of the situation and accepting it, it is possible to get your whole class to support Paul in finding better ways to deal with his anger and everyone can learn about how to express their anger in the process. I think the key is your acceptance of the situation—that means both accepting what happened and accepting your feelings about what happened and then moving on from there to see what learning opportunities open up for all of you.

Please take this suggestion simply as that. If it doesn't feel like an appropriate approach to you, don't try it. It is your class and you—being in the class—know best what may or may not work. I like how you are using the ideas in the book for support.

March 23

I used the advice about bringing up the boys' conflict at our class meeting. I spoke with them both first about how they felt about discussing it with the other children. They were both very open to the idea. In Paul's letter to Can he said, "I am so sorry for fighting with you, but sometimes I am so angry I don't know what to do." We decided to brainstorm a list of positive things we can do when we are angry. Paul was our recorder and wrote everything in his Journal. We discussed what Can and Paul could have done differently. All the students had their own stories about being angry at their siblings. They shared solutions that worked for them in the past.

Paul realized he wasn't alone in becoming angry and also found some outlets for his anger; let's just hope he will be using some of these suggestions. He was told to ignore or move away yesterday but did not take this advice. We discussed how I was angry yesterday and how I dealt with my anger. He now knows that anger is a natural emotion, but there are different ways to deal with anger.

March 24

Today was our "Marble Day" and the kids had a great time. Paul and I discussed the suggestions the class came up with about what people can do when they are angry. He did say that ignoring and moving away don't work for him. He said that sometimes it is nicer and easier just to be angry. He also said that talking and listening to others are suggestions that may work.

March 26

Our class meeting began immediately after morning recess and the only agenda item was, "Why are the police here and why can't we use the normal stairs and doors?" My students are old enough to know when things aren't quite right and were very curious. We were told to tell them that there was a strange car in the parking lot and that the police wanted to make sure that there was nothing in the car that could hurt us.

We discussed conflicts in the world and how we are an international school and sometimes we have to be extra careful when conflicts arise in the world. The students asked if there was a war going on and I said, "No, but there is a 'conflict.'" We discussed how we have talks with our peace wheel when we have conflicts and that leaders of different countries must have similar talks when they have conflicts.

The students were most concerned that if the car was stolen, the robbers would come back to school. No one mentioned the fear of a car bomb. We discussed how school is a safe place and the doors are kept locked. I told them that no one could get in to harm them. They had a million "What if?" questions.

April 6

Our class meeting and Social Studies lesson were a little combined today. I displayed suggested lessons for our unit on Water Transportation (including the study of lakes, rivers and oceans). Once again they suggested some neat ideas that I might never have mentioned. One idea was to write a play and the setting would be on a boat. The art teacher said she would help us design a boat to use in our drama area (I don't have a drama area at the moment but will have to make room!). I shared some of the students' suggestions with the art teacher and she now is planning several lessons where the students can make 3D models of boats. Natsuka's Origami lesson was such a hit last quarter that someone suggested making Origami boats.

April 7

Today our class meeting turned into a "Show and Tell." Several students brought in objects from their Easter Holiday that they wanted to share with their friends. Most of the objects were from visits to Lapland in the Arctic Circle. I have never really encouraged show and tell, but I am beginning to see that the students really enjoy sharing. It is also an excellent experience for them to practice speaking in front of an audience.

During our reading lesson, we came to a consensus about what books the students wanted to read this quarter. It was an easy decision; they are all excited about the Titanic novel we have in the room. We decided to read more short stories in class and have chapter books used for book reports.

I am glancing over my notebook and the various activities I have completed. On March 13, I wrote that I felt consensus is "when a group arrives with a decision that everyone agrees upon." I do not know exactly how my definition has changed, but I have learned over the last month that sometimes it is easier to reach a consensus than other times. However, it has not been as difficult as I expected. There are ways to involve students if they are not too excited about an idea (example: becoming a referee in a game you do not really want to participate in).

April 8

Our class meeting today was spent discussing writing activities for the fourth quarter. We discussed a book report and came to a consensus on the due date. It is funny to see that all but two students wanted the latest date suggested. I guess we learn early in life to procrastinate. I did let them know that I will accept papers at an earlier date.

I put an item on the agenda that has been a problem on the playground. The girls have been whispering about classmates and saying unkind things about each other. We talked about how people feel when others whisper behind their backs. We discussed how we should never say anything that we would not want to say to someone's face. It is always this time of the year that the girls start forming little groups and fighting. I was really hoping I wouldn't have to deal with that this year. After the same group asked to use the peace wheel for the third day in a row, I decided we needed to talk about the issue as a group.

April 12

Today at our class meeting we talked about activities we have planned for the fourth quarter. We discussed what a goal is and why we set goals. I copied the "Common Vision" exercise for the students and had them all come up with a goal for the fourth quarter. Ideally this exercise should be used at the beginning of the year, but I decided to use it now because of the timing of this course. Tomorrow we will share our goals and create a class vision for this last quarter of the school year.

April 13

Yesterday wasn't the best day and we did not have time to brainstorm our homework list. When it was time to copy homework (five minutes before the bell rang), they quickly reminded me that they did not work together to create the homework for the night. I was grumpy, in a hurry, and told them that I would let them give their input tomorrow and that I thought they really needed to do some math work and a journal assignment.

Today I apologized for being in a hurry and we discussed assignments for the week. We don't always complete the homework list for the entire week during our class meetings, but we can come back to it the next day. It helps when we do the entire week at once. This way we can make sure there is a balance in all subject areas.

I encouraged students to add items to our posted "agenda" before our class meetings start. Generally they tell me what to add to the list as soon as our meetings start. Either way will work, but I just want them to know that the agenda items are posted and I would like their input, not just mine. I wonder if I should tell them the suggestions could be anonymous? There might be something that is bothering someone but they don't want to be singled out by their classmates during the discussion.

When we shared our visions/goals for fourth quarter, it allowed me a chance to hear where my students think they need to make improvements. Many students listed different subjects they wanted to be better in and we combined these statements to say, "We will help each other to do our best in all subjects. We then looked at the other goals and thought we should add "...and get along nicely with our friends." Our goal for the fourth quarter will be posted tomorrow in the room to read, "We will help each other in all subjects and get along nicely with our friends." I suggested something-I can't remember what now—but the students didn't like it because it wasn't "a third grader's word." I am looking forward to doing this activity the first day of school next year.

April 14

Today we had a productive class meeting. Each quarter we have a "coffee afternoon" where we invite parents to join us for snack, coffee or juice and share something we have been working on in class. My assistant is a dance instructor and has been teaching the children the waltz. I thought it would be fun to have us all get dressed up for a dance and invite the parents in to join us for a dance. There was an overwhelming response of "NO!" It was in unison and heard very clearly! They did not want their parents seeing them dance with a member of the opposite sex.

After a lengthy discussion we decided to have our own private dance, they even requested paper be put over our class door. We can decorate our room and move the chairs to make room for dancing. We decided to have the dance from 1:30 until 2:00 and invite the parents in to join us at 2:00 for presentations of their work and then we could have coffee, snacks and–only if you wanted to–you may dance with your parent or a friend.

We said we would have our dance lesson this afternoon and see how well we did, before we set a date. I said I would like them to be able to dance without counting aloud "1,2,3, turn" and to look at the person's face or eyes. The cutest little Russian boy raised his hand to say he was afraid of girls' eyes. We decided he could look at his partner's forehead.

This afternoon I was so excited when Tuija, an Italian/Finnish student, asked for the wet erase pen to add an item to the agenda. She wrote "Earth Day" and then said she saw it written on her English calendar. I couldn't believe that I had not even thought about Earth Day. I was in charge of all Earth Day events for the last 3 years in the States and I guess, with everything going on in my life, I forgot about it this year. We tried to do a few things to celebrate Earth Day last year but it has never been celebrated at this school as much as in my past schools. I look forward to brainstorming some neat ideas. Maybe even to share something at our Monday morning assembly. I need to go find all my "Earth Day" files now.

April 15

I was very excited when I glanced at the class agenda and noticed two other items had been added this morning. One was "Daily Edit." Several girls asked if the "Daily Edit " (morning work given twice a week) could be a little harder. It was great to hear they wanted to be challenged a little more. They found the work too easy. It is often hard to find a balance when you have such a large population of students with different mother tongues. Looking back at the vocabulary I used this morning, I think the girls were right: it was easy. Sometimes I worry that my expectations are not high enough for my students.

Earth Day was a topic brought up today. I pulled out my Earth Day folder and shared some information about this day with the class. I told them to brainstorm some activities for Earth Day tonight and we would share our thoughts tomorrow. I get so excited about this topic that I couldn't stop talking. I kept finding something else I just had to share.

The other topic up for discussion was the class library. It is just a mess! It makes me feel so disorganized when I look at it; maybe the students feel the same way. The students wanted to come up with a way to keep it tidy. I have a library helper on my "Busy Bee Helper Chart." Unfortunately, these helpers never do their job and I fail to remind them to do their job. We decided to have the library helper pick one friend in the morning and afternoon to spend 5 minutes arranging the book shelves. I felt as if the students were not all with me during this discussion.

I had everyone raise their hand to show there was a consensus and they were actually all awake and in agreement.

April 16

Yesterday the students placed the class library on the agenda but today I put it there again. The library helpers took half the books off the shelves this morning and the 5 minute clean up session lasted almost 20 minutes. We discussed how the helpers could pick one shelf each to try and tidy and we came to a consensus that this would be a good idea. I hope these suggestions work next week.

We had our "Earth Day" talk today. We decided to do a different activity everyday next week related to helping the Earth. The students brainstormed bulletin board ideas and they will decorate a board in the hallway on Monday.

I wrote the word "Stress Log" on the agenda today. The students kept a log of different stressors in their lives for an entire week. I told them that over half of the class shared one stressful situation. Most of the class was stressed out every morning because they thought they would be late for school. I asked them to think of different ways they could reduce this stress and we would discuss them on Monday. I gave an example of choosing your clothes the night before school as one way to speed up the mornings.

The final item on our agenda was "Ira". One of our students broke her leg in two places over the Easter holiday and has been out of school the last two weeks. She will return on Monday but has a cast all the way up to the top of her thigh. We discussed different ways she will need help. We came to a consensus that every day she would have a different helper. This person will be responsible for helping her with her lunch tray and getting her and her books in and out of her taxi each morning. The students really want to ride in the elevator with her. This student is really struggling academically and I am looking forward to spending recess/PE time helping her with any problems she has in school.

April 19

I am still looking to see how my definition of consensus has changed. I believe the general meaning remains the same, but I am now more aware of how important participation is when reaching a consensus. As a teacher, I feel that it is my job to try and reach the students who are often too shy to participate. I am continuing to try and make every child feel that their participation and opinions are important to the group. It is also a great way to see who is with a discussion and who is daydreaming.

April 20

I am continuing to work on recognizing the importance of my own voice during class meetings. It isn't as easy to do as it sounds. It seems that many times I am the only voice out there, while other times I am not active enough in a discussion.

I am still trying to find that "happy medium." I also believe my input varies depending on how important I feel a particular topic is.

I think this leads me into the topic of class control or sharing authority in decision-making–giving the students responsibility for reaching a consensus. I have realized that once you have given students this responsibility, they do not want to give it back. They now realize that their opinions do have influence over decision-making and they are more likely to share their thoughts.

April 26

I have to admit I have a different attitude [about consensus in the classroom]. At first I was very skeptical about how this was all going to work. I envisioned daily meetings that just dragged on and on and no one ever reached a consensus. I wondered, "How will I ever teach with all these class meetings?"

Last night I realized that I had not had a long meeting in a very long time. I think the reason for this is that, when I started with the consensus classroom, I had never really opened certain items up for discussion. After the first two weeks of meetings, most major areas of concern had been discussed (cutting in line, saving seats at lunch).

April 27

I find that the class meetings are allowing my students to fulfill their emotional need to be heard. The last two days the students have just wanted to share an experience and not a problem. I have had to limit the sharing time because they could talk forever!

April 28

We put Lisa's new glasses on the agenda. Lisa started to wear glasses for the first time today. Can shared how he felt when he first starting wearing glasses and talked about how some students had teased him. He told Lisa (jokingly) that he was mad at her for getting glasses because he would no longer be the only genius in the class.

I had identified "authority issues" as an area of concern for me. I am very relieved that all the concerns I had when I started this course have not turned out to be any major issues at all. Once again, I have to admit that I was skeptical at how this all would work. I was "in charge" of the class and was afraid that by giving the students power to make decisions, I would somehow lose control of the class. Instead of losing control, I think I have gained more respect. I feel they appreciate me more now because they see that I value their opinions.

April 29

Today I worked with a group of five ESL [English as a Second Language] students on writing a skit. They are planning to do a short skit aboard a pirate ship.

We are having a lot of fun preparing. Can brought in more pirate props today. As I was working with this small group, we had to do a great deal of decision-making. We had to come to a consensus about several different events as well as the characters we would have. They are doing a super job cooperating. When someone was not in agreement about an event, we usually came up with a better idea. I look forward to seeing the final production!

April 30

I love your "disturbance rule" [see page 47]. It is simple, to the point, and it works. I think this would be a rule to post in everyone's classroom at the start of the year. When I first used this rule, I did mention that some days are different than others. Sometimes it is OK to make more noise than others. Each day may be different and my tolerance for disturbances may change.

May 5

OK, I feel as if I have not been a very good "Consensus Classroom" teacher today. Today in a language arts lesson, the students had to choose a play to read and then decide who was going to read each part. It took a few minutes to come to a consensus on which play each group would read, but they eventually worked it out.

Next, the groups had to decide who was going to read which part. Group 1 and 2 worked it out and got to work. After about 10 minutes, group 3 could not come to a consensus on who would read which part. I wanted this lesson done today and told them we would just draw names. I put each character's name in a hat and they drew and happily went out in the hall to read.

I didn't ask if they agreed to draw characters from a hat, but now that I think back I do not recall any objections. They seemed much happier after they were assigned a character than when they were fighting over who would do what.

May 7

It is Friday afternoon and we just finished our dance and "coffee afternoon." The kids and the parents loved the afternoon!

Monday, it looks as if "table manners" will be the topic of our class meeting. Several girls were grossed out by burping boys who were also picking their noses and kicking them at lunch time. Yuck! I was happy to see that a child put the topic on the agenda.

May 10

I began interviewing my students today with regards to "The Consensus Classroom." It gave me an opportunity to hear how important the daily class meetings, the posting of an agenda, and the process of reaching a consensus has been to the class. I know I have said this many times, but I really do not feel that

I listened to my students very well before establishing a time for class meetings. One student did mention that I was never too busy to talk about something if it was put on the agenda.

Our agenda had six different items on it today. Needless to say we did not have a chance to discuss everything. I did acknowledge each topic and let them know I was aware of the problem and that it will be discussed tomorrow. Today we focused on table manners and had a brief discussion about the use of jump ropes on the playground. I enjoyed hearing students at lunch remind their friends when they noticed poor table manners.

May 11

During our class meeting we discussed why the third grade students are no longer allowed to use the small play park during recess. We have been using the neighborhood park during our recess period. Pre-Kindergarten through fifth grade all share the field and the play park area at the same time. Pre-K, K, 1st, 2nd and 3rd grade have all been allowed to use the play park area of the field. A neighbor near the school complained that it was too crowded and it was decided that 3rd graders are no longer allowed to use the play park.

I listened to them tell me why they thought 3rd graders should be allowed to use the small park area (it is the only area outside with swings, slides and sand). I recorded everything they said and told them that tomorrow, I will ask for suggestions or solutions to the problem, and then we can submit our complaints and suggestions to the principal and the headmaster on Monday. We have no school on Thursday and Friday this week. Yippee!

I have the class divided into groups of 4 or 5 to work on their skits. I have enjoyed seeing the students use the consensus process in small groups. We discussed that everyone must be in agreement about all ideas. I noticed two girls who did not want to go along with an idea and I told them that was fine, but they must offer some other ideas. They did not take long to find another idea that they were all happy with.

May 17

Today we completed "The Listening Game" [see p. 56]. I had a great deal of information to share about upcoming events and thought this exercise might help keep the students alert. First we took a class quiz on the rules to the game. Next, I shared the announcements and they then took a true or false quiz. Stepan graded the quizzes and everyone received a hundred except Ira. I did not single her out as the person who did not pass, but instead made sure she was listening during our review of the answers. After I reviewed the answers the class earned a marble because they all did well. They enjoyed the activity and it saved me time repeating announcements and instructions.

I had three students visit the principal this morning to voice their concerns about the play park. They had written all the concerns and suggestions down on paper. She said she would meet with the headmaster tomorrow and share what she was told by the third graders. She also said she would call the city (it is a city-run park) and see if 8 year old children are allowed to play in the park. I am pretty happy about how they are having their concerns recognized. Even if everything does not work out, they know they were heard.

May 24

Today I had several students tell me they had something to share at our class meeting. I had to remind them to place their names on the agenda. Today our meeting was a show and tell of sorts. I like having the agenda posted. Now I don't have to worry about kids always asking if they can share something.

I have mentioned earlier that one of my students has a personal aide. Before I began holding class meetings, she would have her snack each day in the teachers' lounge. Once we began our class meetings, she has wanted to remain in class during our snack time. When interviewing the students about how they felt about the consensus classroom, I asked her what she thought and she only had wonderful things to say. She said it was an excellent way to help kids solve problems, to see others' points of view, and to have a place to talk about anything.

June 1

I had recess duty today and was happy to see that six new jump ropes had been purchased. The principal saw that we had more after my students met with her. I am starting to think their voice is more powerful than mine! I think I had mentioned we needed some a while back.

June 4

Yesterday was the best field trip I ever had. I really dreaded taking the kids swimming but it was something that they managed to talk me into doing. The PE teacher joined us on this "Marble Day" trip and has asked me to do it again next year. She told me about ten times how this was the perfect trip and the best field trip she had been on with students. The kids were wonderful and we had great weather, which is a blessing in Finland! It makes a world of difference when you have only 14 students in your class. I am very lucky!! Once again, this was an event that was brought on by a class meeting.

Our class meeting today was rather entertaining. Three boys asked if they could perform a dance. They called themselves the "Cool Dudes." They put on glasses, coats, and baseball caps, and performed the funniest dance. We all had a great laugh. I am starting to tear down my bulletin boards and am ready for summer! Four more days until my vacation!

REFERENCES

Ashton-Warner, Sylvia (1963). *Teacher.* New York: Simon and Schuster.

Berquist, William (1993). *The postmodern organization.* San Francisco: Jossey-Bass Publishers.

Bloom, Benjamin, David Krathwohl, and Masia Bertram (1964). *Taxonomy of educational objectives handbook II: Affective domain.* New York: David McKay Company, Inc.

Brookfield, Stephen (1986). *Understanding and facilitating adult learning.* San Francisco: Jossey-Bass Publishers.

Brown, Molly Y. (1993). *Growing whole: Self-realization on an endangered planet.* Mt. Shasta, CA: Psychosynthesis Press.

Brown, Molly Y. (2004). *Unfolding Self: The practice of psychosynthesis.* New York: Helios Press.

Bruffee, K. (1993). *Collaborative learning: higher education, interdependence, and the authority of knowledge.* Baltimore: John Hopkins University Press.

Butler, C.T. (1987). *On conflict and consensus.* Food Not Bombs Publishing. www.consensus.net

Caine, Renate N. and Geoffrey Caine (1994). *Making connections: Teaching and the human brain.* Menlo Park, CA: Addison-Wesley Publishing Company.

Capra, Fritjof. (1996). *The web of life.* New York: Anchor Press.

Cell, Edward (1984). *Learning to learn from experience.* Albany: State University of New York Press.

Charney, Ruth Sidney (1991). *Teaching children to care: Management in the responsive classroom.* Greenfield, MA: Northeast Foundation for Children.

Consensus Classroom, Inc. (2000). *Consensus classroom* (video). Santa Rosa, CA: Consensus Classroom, Inc.

Crosby, R.P. (1998). *The authentic leader: How authority and consensus intertwine.* Seattle, WA: Skaya Publishing.

Daloz, Laurent A. (1986). *Effective teaching and mentoring: Realizing the transformational power of adult learning experiences.* San Francisco: Jossey-Bass Publishers.

Development Studies Center (1996). *Ways we want our class to be: Class meetings that build commitment to kindness and learning.* Oakland CA: Development Studies Center.

Dewey, John (1938). *Experience and education.* New York: Collier Macmillan Publishers.

Doll, William (1993). *A post-modern perspective on curriculum.* New York: Teachers College Press.

Flake, Carol L. (1993). *Holistic education: Principles, perspectives, and practices.* Vermont: Holistic Education Press.

Freire, Paulo (1997). *Pedagogy of the oppressed.* New York: Continuum.

Gang, Phil (1989). *Rethinking education.* Vermont: Dagaz Press.

Gardner, Howard (1983). *Frames of mind: The theory of multiple intelligences.* New York: Basic Books.

Gibbs, Jeanne (1994). *Tribes: A new way of learning together.* Santa, Rosa, California: Center Source Publications.

Glasser, William (1998). *Choice theory: A new psychology of personal freedom.* New York: HarperCollins Publishers, Inc.

Goldberger, Nancy, Jill Tarule, Blythe Clinchy, and Mary Belenky (1996). *Knowledge, difference, and power.* New York: Harper Collins Publishers.

Gordon, Thomas (1974). *T.E.T.: Teacher effectiveness training.* New York: David McKay Company.

hooks, bell (1994). *Teaching to transgress: Education as the practice of freedom.* New York: Routledge.

Hunter, D., A. Bailey and B. Taylor. (1997) *Co-operacy: A new way of being at work.* Fisher Books.

Kagan, Dr. Spencer (1994). *Cooperative learning.* San Juan Capistrano, CA: Kagan Cooperative Learning.

Kohn, Alfie (1992). *No contest: The case against competition.* Boston: Houghton Mifflin Company.

Kohn, Alfie (1993). *Punished by rewards: The trouble with gold stars, incentive plans, A's, praise, and other bribes.* Boston: Houghton Mifflin Company.

Laszlo, Evin. (1972). *The systems view of the world.* New York: Braziller.

Maslow, Abraham H. (1968). *Toward a psychology of being.* New York: D. Van Nostrand Company.

Maslow, Abraham H. (1976). *The farther reaches of human nature.* New York: Penguin Books.

Macy, Joanna & Molly Young Brown. (1998) *Coming back to life: Practices to reconnect our lives, our world.* Gabriola Island, BC: New Society Publishers.

Macy, Joanna. (1991). *Mutual causality in Buddhism and General Systems Theory: The dharma of natural systems.* Buffalo, NY: SUNY Press.

Mezirow, Jack (1991). *Transformative dimensions of adult learning.* San Francisco: Jossey-Bass Publishers.

Nelsen, Jane (1996), *Positive discipline.* New York: Ballantine Books.

Noddings, Nel (1992). *The challenge to care in schools: An alternative approach to education.* New York: Teachers College Press.

Palmer, Parker J. (1998). *The courage to teach: Exploring the inner landscape of a teacher's life.* San Francisco: Jossey-Bass Publishers.

Rogers, Carl (1961). *On becoming a person.* New York: Houghton Mifflin.

Rogers, Carl (1977). *On personal power: Inner strength and its revolutionary impact.* New York: Delta Publishing Co.

Saint, S. and J.R.Lawson. (1994). *Rules for reaching consensus: A modern approach to decision making.* Amsterdam: Pfeiffer & Company.

Sartor, Linda (1998). *Collaboration and how to facilitate it: A cooperative inquiry.* Dissertation Abstracts International, 58 (11), 441 (University Microfilms No. 9814533).

Schaps, Eric (June, 1990). Cooperative learning: The challenge in the '90s. *Cooperative Learning.* pp. 5-8.

Scott, J. and E. Flanigan (1996). *Achieving consensus: Tools and techniques.* Menlo Park, CA: Crisp Publications, Inc.

Tagliere, D.A. (1993). *How to meet, think, and work to consensus.* San Diego, CA: Pfeiffer & Company.

Whipple, W. (1987). Collaborative learning: Recognizing it when we see it. *AAHE Bulletin,* 40 (2), 3-7.

Index

Academic performance, 12–13, 84–85
Agreement, 9, 10, 16
   by everyone, 9, 10
Agreements, 21
   file or list of, 46
   keeping agreements, 35, 37
Arguments, 48
Ashton-Warner, Sylvia, 70
Assumptions, 61, 66, 68, 69, 70, 73, 94
Audubon Expedition Institute, 1, 27
Authenticity, 64
Authority, 5, 15, 23, 24, 30, 32, 36, 61, 62–64, 93, 114
   inner authority, 23
   shared authority, 9, 21–25, 32, 51, 52, 61, 62–64, 90–92, 114
Belenky, Mary, 72
Belonging, 34, 35
Blocking decision, 12, 37, 89, 90.
Brain research, 12, 13, 66, 67, 97
Brainstorming, 31, 44, 47, 50, 55, 86, 103, 105
Brookfield, Stephen, 68
Caine, Renate N. & Geoffrey, 67
Caring, 25, 35, 51, 71–72, 74, 76, 77
Cell, Edward, 63
Changing behavior, 37
Charney, Ruth, 64, 65, 71, 76
Choice, 65–66
Civil disobedience, 1, 51, 52
Class meetings, 43–46, 75, 76–77, 76, 87–88, 99–101
   agenda, 30, 32, 35, 36, 43–45, 57, 87, 101–102, 110
   decision-making, 45-46
   leadership, 22
Clinchy, Blythe, 72
Cohousing, 2, 10, 90
Collaboration, 4, 62, 65, 77
Coming Back to Life, 2
Common vision, 34, 35, 85, 89–90, 109
Communication, 12, 15, 26, 28, 33, 47, 49, 61, 68, 71, 84, 99, 107
Community, 38
   conscious community, 21, 33–35, 37
   consensus, 1
   learning community, 1, 43, 61, 70, 73–74, 76, 77
Compromise, 10
Conflict resolution, 49, 104
Consensus
   "stand aside", 10
   "stuck in the muck", 90
   checking for agreement, 10, 38
   decisions on school work, 30–32
   introducing, 85–89
   majority vote within consensus, 47
   meaning of, 9–11, 113
   problems with, 2, 11–12, 89–90
   resources, 95
   skills, 11, 23, 25, 101
Consensus Classroom, Inc, 2, 98, 116

Consequences, 5, 26, 36, 44, 46, 48, 50, 51, 52, 54, 56, 76, 90
Cooperation, 11, 69, 70, 75
Court system, 22, 33, 34, 43, 50–52, 53
Creative decision-making, 21, 32–33
Creative solutions, 15, 33
Creativity, 9, 21, 32, 33, 76
Daloz, Lawrence, 71, 72
Democracy, 5, 21, 62, 64-65, 94
Dewey, John, 61, 62, 66, 67
Discussion
    colored cards, 12
Disturbance rule, 47–49, 53, 93, 115
Diversity, 3, 17, 25, 61, 74, 77
Doll, William, 61, 68, 69, 70
Environmental education, 1, 61
Everyone's concerns, 16, 92
Everyone's needs, 10, 16, 21, 23, 25, 47
Facilitating Collaboration, 1
Facilitator, 2, 11, 12, 46, 77
Feedback, 16, 22, 29, 31, 35, 36, 37, 55, 74, 90
Feelings, 12, 24, 26–27, 28, 38, 93
Freire, Paulo, 63, 67, 68
Gang, Phil, 64
Gibbs, Jeanne, 74, 75, 77
Glasser, William, 65
Goals, 34, 35, 77, 88, 109, 110
Goldberger, Nancy, 72
Homework, 32, 54–55, 102, 103, 109
    consensus decisions about, 32, 54–55, 85, 86–87

hooks, bell, 72, 73, 74
Inquiry, 61, 63, 66, 67, 77
Interpersonal conflicts, 23–25, 28, 33, 43, 50
Kagan, Spencer, 64, 74, 75, 76
Kohn, Alfie, 62, 65, 66, 74, 75, 76
Learning
    cooperative, 74–76
    transformative, 68
Linda's voice, 4
Listening, 5, 10, 23, 24, 25, 35, 36, 38, 44, 49, 69, 71, 72, 86, 100, 102, 108
    the listening game, 56, 114
Love, 28–29
Majority rule, 2, 9, 11, 13, 15, 16, 32, 76, 78
Majority vote
    within consensus, 47
Meeting school requirements, 17, 21, 44, 67, 84, 86, 87
Mezirow, Jack, 63, 68
Money system, 22, 32, 33, 34, 44, 52–54
Multiculturalism, 72
Name-calling, 37, 49–50
Nelsen, Jane, 76
Noddings, Nel, 71
Palmer
    Parker, 63, 64
Paradigm shift, 13, 43, 61, 68, 73, 75, 90
Participation, 15, 21, 29–32, 35, 62, 64, 76, 77, 89, 99, 100, 112
Pearce, Joseph Chilton, 12-13

Pedagogy, 72, 73
Personal responsibility, 35, 66
Playing favorites, 48
Post-Modernism, 61–62, 69, 70, 77
Power differentials, 12
Power struggles, 21, 23, 24–25, 33, 91
Power-over & power-with, 25
Praxis, 67, 68
Problem-solving, 10, 76
Punishment, 30, 32, 65, 107
Put-downs, 12, 37, 48, 49–50
Quakers, 1, 9, 10
Rewards, 52, 65, 66, 74, 117
Schaps, Eric, 76
Self-expression, 21, 25–29, 32, 49, 92–93
Self-organizing, 15, 70
Self-regulating, 15
Speaking up, 12, 21, 23, 25, 27–28, 33, 35, 36, 37, 38, 44, 45, 47, 93, 99, 101
Spontaneity, 37, 38, 67, 92
Student leadership, 22
Students as teachers, 22
Synergy, 10, 14, 15, 16, 34
Systems theory, 13–17
    adaptation, 14, 15, 16
    emergent properties, 14
    General Systems Theory, 13
    holonarchy, 14, 15
    nested hierarchy, 14
    homeostasis, 14, 15, 16
    invariants, 14, 15, 16
    requisite variety, 17
    subsidiarity, 16
    synergy, 14, 15, 16, 34
Tarule, Jill, 72, 73
Tattling, 48
Teasing, 29
Testing, standardized, 85
The Consensus Classroom, 2, 105, 106
Time use, 11–12, 84, 101
    "the inevitable long meeting," 89
Trust, 21, 23, 25, 26, 27, 33, 37, 71
Victim, being a, 25
Voice, 29, 71–72, 73
Women's Ways of Knowing, 72, 73
Yurt circle, 30, 85–86

More Books from Psychosynthesis Press
By Molly Young Brown

GROWING WHOLE: Self-Realization on an Endangered Planet. Offering direct access to the powerful tools of psychosynthesis, this self-study guide is for people seeking to live more creative and meaningful lives, and to contribute to an Earth-saving transformation of consciousness.
(Psychosynthesis Press, 1997. ISBN 0-9611444-1-6 $12)

GROWING WHOLE: Exploring the Wilderness Within. A workshop-in-a-box, for discovering your strengths, creativity, and wisdom. Listen to the author's voice (on audiocassette or CD) guide you through meditations and inner dialogues. A structured journal includes step-by-step exercises–both writing and drawing–to develop self-awareness, strengthen your center, and activate your talents.
(Psychosynthesis Press, 1997. ISBN 0-9611444-2-4 $15 for audiocassette version, $17 for CD version)

Books by Molly Brown from other publishers

COMING BACK TO LIFE: Practices to Reconnect Our Lives, Our World (co-authored with Joanna Macy). With eloquent and compelling insight into the roots of our angst, the authors point the way forward out of apathy to "the work that reconnects," as developed by Joanna Macy and her colleagues over the last 20 years. All those concerned with peace, spirit, education, and eco-activism find here an inspiring and practical guide.
(New Society, 1998. ISBN 0-86571-391-X $16.95)

UNFOLDING SELF: The Practice of Psychosynthesis. A revised updated edition of a classic text on psychosynthesis counseling and psychotherapy, for counselors, therapists, life coaches, and teachers who want to challenge their clients and students to more fully use their creative and healing powers. It also offers guidance to anyone engaged in a program of self-discovery.
(Helios/Allworth Press, September, 2004)

Ordering Information
Order these books through your local independent bookstore or directly from:
Psychosynthesis Press
PO Box 1301
Mt Shasta CA 96067
(530) 926-0986
www.mollyyoungbrown.com/books.htm
books@MollyYoungBrown.com.

Psychosynthesis Press books are available at volume and trade discounts to organizations and bookstores.

www.ingramcontent.com/pod-product-compliance
Lightning Source LLC
Chambersburg PA
CBHW051212290426
44109CB00021B/2428